Meditations for Advent

Jacques-Bénigne Bossuet

Meditations for Advent

Translated by Christopher O. Blum

SOPHIA INSTITUTE PRESS

Manchester, New Hampshire

Meditations for Advent is a translation of *Élévations à Dieu sur tous les mystères de la religion chrétienne*, from *Oeuvres complètes de Bossuet*, edited by Abbé Guillaume and published by Briday in Lyon, France, in 1879.

Sophia Institute Press
Box 5284, Manchester, NH 03108
1-800-888-9344

www.SophiaInstitute.com

Sophia Institute Press® is a registered trademark of Sophia Institute.

Library of Congress Cataloging-in-Publication Data

Bossuet, Jacques Bénigne, 1627-1704.
  [Élévations à Dieu sur tous les mystères de la religion chrétienne. English. Selections]
  Meditations for Advent / Jacques-Bénigne Bossuet ; translated by Christopher O. Blum.
      p. cm.
  Includes bibliographical references.
  ISBN 978-1-933184-87-6 (pbk. : alk. paper) 1. Meditations. I. Blum, Christopher Olaf, 1969- II. Title.
  BX2183.B6313 2012
  242'.332—dc23

                                                                          2012031204

Contents

Foreword

Every year our holy mother the Church invites us to make our way back to Bethlehem. And when we arrive, what is it that we see there? Nothing but "three poor people who love one another," as the poet Claudel said, but three poor people who "will change the face of the earth."[1]

There is great wisdom in the Church's setting aside as holy that month of expectation that is the liturgical season of Advent. For, like the Holy Family, we too are poor. Yet we are poor in the very way that they were rich, and rich in the way that they were poor. And this is why we sorely need Advent as an annual occasion to listen to the prophet Isaiah, to marvel at the Annunciation, the Visitation, and the birth of Saint John the Baptist, to enter more deeply into the meaning of those two great songs of faith that frame the Church's daily prayer, the *Benedictus* and the *Magnificat*, and to join Saint Joseph and the

[1] Paul Claudel, *Toi, qui es-tu?* (Paris: Gallimard, 1936), 54.

Blessed Virgin in silent adoration of the incarnate Son of God. For just such an Advent journey of contemplation, this slim volume is an admirable *vade mecum*. In it you will find a distillation of the doctrine and the piety of an eloquent preacher and a man of deep and weighty prayer.

The days are not so long ago when the figure of Jacques-Bénigne Bossuet (1627-1704) needed no introduction and when the very thought of translating his sublime French into English would have been considered an impertinence. But we no longer live in the world of Monsignor Knox and Mr. Waugh—and certainly not that of Mr. Belloc—a world in which it could be taken for granted that educated men and women read French and that educated Catholics read the right sort of French authors. And so there is another task of *ressourcement* that must be undertaken, a reclaiming of an inheritance, one of whose central figures is the Eagle of Meaux, as the great Bossuet was called, after the name of his bishopric and for his clear vision and elevated style.

Born to an industrious and dignified Burgundian family, Bossuet labored mightily in the vineyard of the Word, as a preacher should. He knew the Scriptures by heart. He read and reread the Fathers, chiefly Saint Augustine. He made his own the doctrine of the Church, especially as transmitted by Saint Thomas Aquinas. With his inimitable craft, he put this solid learning to work, producing monuments of French style such as the funeral orations for the princess Henriette-Marie and the great Condé and becoming the schoolmaster not only of the dauphin, son of the *Roi Soleil*, but of generations of Catholics in *la belle France* and wherever the French tongue was read. His *Discourse on Universal History* and *History of the Variations of the Protestant Churches* cast a long shadow, shaping minds as varied as Joseph de Maistre and T. S. Eliot, Christopher Dawson, and Paul Claudel.

The work here at hand is a careful selection of forty daily meditations—sufficient to stretch from Thanksgiving into the Octave of Christmas—taken from a much longer work, the *Élévations à Dieu sur tous les mystères de la religion chrétienne*. The first word of this title defeats easy translation, although its meaning is plain enough. These are texts meant to assist the Christian in the difficult task of lifting the mind to the consideration of God. The notion here is one common to the French School of spirituality that descends from Pierre de Bérulle: that the omnipotent and eternal God is not like us, but because of his infinite condescension in becoming man, we are apt to think that he is. And so, as an astute commentator on Bossuet has said, these meditations spring in part from the author's conviction that "the majority of our errors in the Christian life and particularly in the life of devotion arise from our failure sufficiently to respect God, from our failure to esteem him highly enough."[2] It is Bossuet's lofty sense of God's grandeur that gives us the sonorous meditations on the Creation, on the Word, and on the priesthood of Jesus Christ. Yet the same Bossuet who was heir to the austere theological vision of Cardinal de Bérulle was equally the follower of the mild Saint Francis de Sales and the charitable Saint Vincent de Paul. So here too we find stirring calls to poverty, silence, and simplicity of life within the context of reflections on the Blessed Virgin and—in one of the earliest and most celebrated examples of its kind—a sermon in appreciation of the holy patriarch Saint Joseph.

The Father, as we are told by the Incarnate Word himself, seeks souls who will adore him "in spirit and in truth" (John 4:23). There is work enough here for both heart and mind, and these gleanings from Bossuet's harvest of the French School of spirituality are trustworthy help for the task.

Romanus Cessario, O.P.

[2] Jean Calvet, *La littérature religieuse de François de Sales à Fénelon* (Paris: Del Duca, 1956), 314-315.

Prayer to Jesus Christ

Jesus, my Savior, true God and true man, and the true Christ promised to the patriarchs and the prophets from the beginning of the world and, in time, faithfully bestowed to the holy people you had chosen, you have said by your holy and divine mouth: "This is eternal life, that they know thee the only true God, and Jesus Christ whom thou hast sent" (John 17:3). Believing in these words, and with the help of your grace, I wish to be attentive to the task of knowing God and knowing you.

So do I draw as near to you as I can, with a lively faith, to know God in you and by you, and to know him in a manner worthy of God—that is, in a manner that leads me to love and to obey him, in accord with the words of your beloved disciple: "He who says 'I know him' but disobeys his commandments is a liar" (1 John 2:4), as well as your very own: "He who has my commandments and keeps them, he it is who loves me" (John 14:21).

Meditations for Advent

To know you well, O my God and dear Savior, I wish always, with the help of your grace, to contemplate you in all that befalls you and in all of your mysteries, and at the same time to know your Father, who gave you to us, and the Holy Spirit that you both have sent to us. So do I wish to love you with true faith, a "faith working through love" (Gal. 5:6). Amen.

Meditations for Advent

1

The Creation of the Universe

Recollected within myself, seeing in myself only sin, imperfection, and nothingness, I see at the same time above me a happy and perfect nature, and I say to him within myself with the psalmist: "You are my God; you have no need of my possessions" (cf. Ps. 16:2), for you have no need of any possessions.

"I AM WHO I AM [Exod. 3:14]. My existence suffices; all the rest is of no use to me." Yes, Lord, all the rest is of no use to you and contributes nothing to your greatness. You are no greater with the whole world, or with a thousand millions of worlds, than you are alone. When you made the world, it was by your goodness, and not from necessity. It is fitting that you should be able to create all that you please, for it is part of the perfection of your being and of the efficacy of your will not only that you should exist, but that all that you will should exist — that it should exist as soon as you will it, to the extent that you will it, when you will it. And when you will it, you do not begin to will it: from all eternity you will what you will without ever changing. Nothing begins in you, and everything begins outside of you by your eternal order. Is something lacking to you because you do not do as many things as you are able to do? The whole universe you have made is but a little part of what you could have made, and, after all, is as nothing before you. If you had made nothing, existence would be lacking to the things that you had not willed to make. But nothing is lacking to you, because independent of all things, you are the one who is, and who is everything that it is necessary to be in order to be perfect and happy.

O Father eternal and independent of all things! Your Son and your Holy Spirit are with you; you have no need of society, for here is a society in yourself that is eternal and inseparable from you. You are content with this infinite and eternal communication of your perfect and blessed essence to these two Persons who are equal to you, who are not at all your work, but who are your cooperators; who are like you, not by your commandment, or by an effect of your omnipotence, but by the sole perfection and plenitude of your being. Every other communication is incapable of adding anything to your greatness, to your perfection, to your happiness.

The Creation of the Universe

God said: "Let there be light, and there was light" (Gen. 1:3). The king says, "Let them march," and the army marches, or "Let such and such be done," and it is accomplished; a whole army stirs at a single word from the prince—that is to say, from the merest movement of his lips. This is the most excellent image of the power of God among human things, but, in the end, it is a defective one. God does not move his lips. God does not strike the air with his tongue to draw forth some sound. God has only to will inside himself, and all that he wills eternally is accomplished as he wills it and in the time he has marked out.

And so he said let there be light, and it was; let there be a firmament, and there was one; let the waters be gathered, and they were gathered; let two great lights be illuminated, and they lit up; let animals come forth, and they came forth. "For he spoke, and it came to be; he commanded, and it stood forth" (Ps. 32:9). There is "none that can resist his voice" (Jdt. 16:14). The shadow does not follow the body any faster than all things follow the commandment of the Almighty.

O God, how poor is my soul! It is truly nothingness from which, little by little, you draw forth the good with which you wish to fill it; it is naught but chaos, before you have begun to untangle all its thoughts. When you make the light dawn within it through faith, it remains imperfect until you have formed it by charity, and you, who are the true sun of justice, as burning as you are luminous, have embraced me with your love! O God, may you be praised forever by your works. It is not enough to have illuminated me once; without your help I would fall again into my initial darkness. The air needs the sun to illuminate it; how much more do I need you ceaselessly to illuminate me. Ever my prayer should be: "Let there be light!"

2

The Creation and Fall
of the Angels

God, who is a pure spirit, wished to create pure spirits like himself, spirits who, like him, live with intelligence and love, and who are blessed in knowing and loving him as he is happy in knowing and loving himself, and thus carry in their very bosom a divine character by which they are made in his image and likeness.

These most perfect creatures were drawn forth from nothingness like all others and, although perfect, they are fallible by their nature. The one who is by his nature infallible is the one who comes from himself and who is perfect in his essence. As he is the only perfect thing; everything except him is defective: "Even in his servants he puts no trust, and his angels he charges with error" (Job 4:18).

He is not, however, the one who caused their error. Nothing but the very best comes from so good and powerful a hand. All of the spirits are pure in their origin; all these intelligent beings were holy in their creation, for in them God at once formed their nature and poured out his grace upon them.

Everything can change, except God. "Behold, God puts no trust in his holy ones, and the heavens are not clean in his sight" (Job 15:15). Those he created to serve him were not stable; "and his angels he charges with error." A friend of Job said this and was not rebuked by that irreproachable man. It was the common doctrine of the whole world, in conformity with this thought: "God," said Saint Peter, "did not spare the angels when they sinned, but cast them into hell and committed them to pits of nether gloom to be kept until the judgment" (2 Peter 2:4). And Jesus Christ himself said, speaking of Satan, "there is no truth in him" (John 8:44).

"How are you fallen from heaven, O Day Star?" (Isa. 14:12). You carried in yourself "the signet of perfection, full of wisdom and perfect in beauty" (Ezek. 28:12). You had with you all the sanctified spirits in the paradise of our God, "every precious stone was your covering" (Ezek. 28:13), the brilliance and ornament of grace. Like a cherubim with outstretched wings, you shone "on the holy mountain of God; in the midst of the stones of fire you walked, blameless in your ways from the day you were created, till iniquity was found in you" (Ezek. 28:14-15). How was it found there? By what path did it enter? Was error able to insinuate itself amid so much clarity, or depravity and iniquity amid such great graces? Truly, everything that is drawn forth from nothingness holds to it always. He was sanctified, but he was not holy like God; he was at first ruled, but not like God, whose very will is his rule.

One of his beauties is that he was endowed with a free will, but not like God's free will, which is indefectible. This proud and wretched spirit made himself his own end; admiring his own beauty, he became a snare to himself, saying, "I will ascend above the heights of the clouds, I will make myself like the Most High" (Isa. 14:14). This high creature desired an elevation other than the one proper to him: he wished to be like God, together with the other spirits he seduced into imitating his pride. And all at once he was "brought down" and cast into "the depths of the pit" (Isa. 14:15), where we who are on the earth see him. There was no other cause of his defection than his own will.

O you proud and rebellious men, take heed of the example of the prince of rebellion and pride. See and consider what a single instance of pride did in him and in all of his followers.

Let us flee, let us flee from ourselves. Let us recall our nothingness. Let us find in God our whole foundation, and let us place all our love in him. Amen. Amen.

3

The Perseverance of the Holy Angels

"Now war arose in heaven, Michael and his angels fighting against the dragon; and the dragon and his angels fought, but they were defeated and there was no longer any place for them in heaven" (Rev. 12:7-8).

What kind of war was this? What were the weapons of those spiritual powers? "For we are not contending against flesh and blood, but against ... the spiritual hosts of wickedness in the heavenly places" and in "the present darkness" that surrounds us (Eph. 6:12).

We must not imagine this war as having been one of bodily arms or material weapons, nor of bloodshed, as it is among us: it was a conflict of thoughts and affections. The angel of pride, who is called the dragon, raised his army of angels and said to them: "We are happy in ourselves, and like God, we shall do our own will." And Michael contradicted him, saying: "Who is like God? Who can make himself equal to him?" From this comes the name *Michael*, which means "Who is like God?" Can there be any doubt that the name of God will triumph in this war? What can the weak spirits — weak because they are proud—what can they accomplish against the humble army that the Lord has rallied behind him? They fall from the heavens, and their place, once so great, is empty. What ravages have been done by their desertion! But these vast spaces will not remain vacant, for God will create man to fill up the places left empty by their treason. Flee, wretched army. Who is like God? Flee before Michael and the holy angels.

Thus were the heavens purified: the haughty spirits were banished from it forever. Neither revolt, nor pride, nor dissension has any place there. It is a Jerusalem, a city of peace, where the holy angels are united to God and "always behold the face of the Father" (cf. Matt. 18:10). Assured of their happiness, they wait with submission for the renewal of their ranks that will come from the earth.

Be happy, holy angels. Come to our aid. May the innumerable armies of the enemy perish in a single night by the same hand that slew the firstborn of Egypt, the persecutor of the people of God (Exod. 12:29).

Holy angel, whoever you may be, to whom God has entrusted me, throw back those proud tempters who, continuing their war against God, struggle with him for the man that is his conquest and try to make off with him.

The Perseverance of the Holy Angels

O Saint Michael, powerful protector of the holy people, whose prayers you offer to God like incense (Rev. 8:3), let me endlessly join you in saying, "Who is like God?" O Saint Gabriel, you who were called the strength of God, who brought to Mary tidings of the coming of Christ, whose future arrival you had foretold to Daniel, inspire us with holy thoughts so that we may profit from your predictions. O Saint Raphael, whose name means "the physician of God," heal my soul of a more dangerous blindness than that which afflicted the holy man Tobit; bind the demon of impurity that attacks the sons of Adam even within the holiness of marriage; bind him, for you are more powerful than he, and God himself is your strength. Holy Angels, all of you "ministering servants" who see the face of God (Heb. 1:14) and whom he has commanded "to guard us in all our ways" (cf. Ps. 91:11), use the aids God has given you for the salvation of his elect, and raise up our weakness.

O God, send us your holy angels: those who served Jesus Christ after his fast, those who guarded his sepulcher and announced his Resurrection, those who comforted him in his agony. Jesus Christ had no need of this help; he had but clothed himself with our weakness. We are the infirm members that the consoling angel came to fortify in the person of their head.

4

The Creation of Man

"Thou hast made him little less than the angels, and dost crown him with glory and honor. Thou hast given him dominion over the works of thy hands" (Ps. 8:5-6). So David sang in memory of the creation of man. And it is true: man, united to a body, is inferior to these pure spirits, but only a little beneath, for, like them, he has life and intelligence and love, and he is made happy by what makes them happy. God is the common happiness of each; and, in this regard equal to the angels, their brothers and not their subjects, we are only a little less than they.

You have crowned him with honor and glory, according to his soul and according to his body. You have given him justice, the original righteousness, immortality, and dominion over all bodily creatures. The angels, lacking bodies, have no need for these creatures, which confer no good upon them. Yet God has placed man in this sensible and corporeal world to contemplate it and to enjoy it. To contemplate it, according to the words of David, "I look at thy heavens, the work of thy fingers, the moon and the stars which thou hast established" (Ps. 8:3), amid the immense night sky that envelops them in their courses and is ruled by a law of inviolable stability. Man should also enjoy the world, according to the usages that God has prescribed for it: of the sun, the moon, and the stars, "for signs and for seasons and for days and years" (Gen. 1:14). All the rest of corporeal nature is submitted to his empire. He cultivates the earth and makes it fertile. He makes the seas serve his purposes and commerce. All the animals recognize his rule, either because they fear him or because he employs them to his various ends. But sin has weakened this empire and has left us only a miserable remnant of it.

As everything was to have been put into the power of man, God created man after all the rest, introducing him into the universe as one introduces into a room the one in whose honor the party is being held, after everything is ready and when the dinner is served. Man is the perfect complement to the other works of God, and after having made him as his masterpiece, God rested.

"Let us make man in our image and likeness" (cf. Gen. 1:26). At these words, the image of the Trinity begins to appear. It shines magnificently in the rational creature.

Like the Father, man has being; like the Son, he has intelligence; like the Holy Spirit, he has love. Like the Blessed Trinity, he has in his being and his intelligence and his love, one same happiness and life. There is no way to take one from him without taking them all. Happy creature, and perfectly similar to God, if he would concern himself only with God. Then, perfect in his being, intelligence, and love, he would understand all that he is and love all that he understood. His being and its operations would be inseparable; God would become the perfection of his being, the immortal food of his intelligence, life, and love. Like God, he would say but one single word, which would comprehend all his wisdom; like God, he would produce one sole love, which would embrace all his good, and all of this would be undying in him. Grace comes in above this foundation and lifts up nature. Glory is shown to him and adds to his complement of grace. Happy creature once again, if only he knew how to preserve this happiness!

But man has lost it. O man, where did your intelligence go astray? To what objects has your love descended? Alas! Return to your source.

5

The Fall of Man

"Now the serpent was more subtle than any other wild creature" (Gen. 3:1). We see the admirable depth of Christian theology in the apparent weakness of this strange beginning to the story of our woes. The whole tale seems a fable. A serpent speaks. A woman listens. A man so perfect and enlightened allows himself to be led astray by the most common of temptations. All mankind falls with him into sin and death. It seems to be so much foolishness. Yet we have that sublime saying of Saint Paul: "The foolishness of God is wiser than men, and the weakness of God is stronger than men" (1 Cor. 1:25).

Let us begin with the subtlety of the serpent, not regarding it as the subtlety of an irrational animal, but as the subtlety of the Devil, who entered into the body of this animal by divine permission.

Just as God appeared to man under a sensible form, so also did the angels. God spoke to Adam. God led the animals to him, and he brought him the wife that he had just formed from his side. God appeared to him as someone walking in paradise. In all these appearances there was an exterior shape. As man is composed of body and soul, so God made himself known by both, that is, by senses and intellect. It was the same with the angels whom God allowed to converse with man under the forms of animals. Eve was not surprised to hear a serpent speak. She knew that an angel was speaking to her, but she was unable to distinguish whether it was a good or an evil one.

"Why did the Lord forbid you to eat the fruit of this tree?" And, a little while later, "You will not die" (Gen. 3:4). The Devil wished to lead Eve into error, but if he had begun by proposing the error into which he wished to lead her—a manifest contradiction of the commandment and the word of God—he would have inspired horror rather than the desire to listen. So he first sowed the seeds of doubt, asking "Why has the Lord forbidden you?" The Devil did not dare to say, "He tricked you," or "His precept is unjust," or "His word is not trustworthy." Rather he inquired, he questioned, as if he wished to be instructed rather than to instruct the one he wanted to suborn. He could not have begun in a more insinuating and subtle manner.

The Fall of Man

When he saw that Eve had been dazzled by novelty and had already consented to the doubt he had suggested, he lost no time in half measures and stated openly: "You will not die. For God knows that when you eat of it your eyes will be opened, and you will be like God, knowing good and evil" (Gen. 3:5). With these words he suggested that God had attached to the fruit of this tree some divine power by which man would know all in matters of good or evil, happiness or wretchedness. And then he said, "You will become like gods." Thus, he flattered pride; he stroked and excited curiosity. When Eve looked upon the forbidden fruit, her disobedience began, for the fruit that God had forbidden to be touched should not even have been looked upon with delight. She saw, the Scriptures say, "that the tree was good for food, and that it was a delight to the eyes" (Gen. 3:6). To make herself so attentive to the beauty and the taste of what had been forbidden was to choose to be seduced.

"She took its fruit and ate; and she also gave some to her husband, and he ate. Then the eyes of both were opened, and they knew that they were naked; and they sewed fig leaves together and made themselves aprons" (Gen. 3:6-7). This expression is a modest and dignified way of saying that they began to know evil. In a word, their minds, which had risen up against God, could no longer compass the bodies that they should have commanded. Immediately after their sin appears the cause of the shame that they had not known until then.

We are all born of Adam and Eve, and that is why our birth—and even our conception, the very source of our being—is tainted by Original Sin.

O God, where are we, and into what sort of condition have we fallen?

6

The First Promise of a Redeemer

It was on the very day of our fall that God said to the serpent, our corrupter: "I will put enmity between you and the woman, and between your seed and her seed; she shall bruise your head" (Gen. 3:15).

One must not think that God desired to judge or to punish the visible serpent, for it is an animal lacking intelligence. This is an allegory in which the serpent is judged as a figure of the Devil, whose instrument he had been. By the seed of the serpent is to be understood all liars, whose father he is, as the Savior explains: "When he lies, he speaks according to his own nature, for he is a liar and the father of lies" (John 8:44). By the seed of the woman is to be understood one of her descendants, a fruit that will come forth from her by which she shall bruise the head of the serpent. One must not suppose that the entire race of women could be victorious over the serpent, seeing as we do so great a number of them who do not ever lift themselves up from their own fall. The seed of the woman triumphs insofar as there is a child of the woman who will defeat the demon and all of his minions.

One of the ancient versions of the text—the one that we follow here—attributes this victory to the woman, saying that it will be "she" who shall bruise his head: *ipsa conteret.* We must understand that the woman will enjoy this victory by means of bringing the victor into the world. In this way, two lessons are joined: the one that we find in the original, which credits the victory to the son of the woman, and the one in our own version, which credits it to the woman herself. So, in whichever way we take the text, we see come forth from the woman a fruit that will crush the head of the serpent and destroy his empire.

If God had not said that there would be an eternal enmity between the serpent and the woman, or with the fruit that she should bear, the future victory of the woman and her son would not have been foretold. Yet we do see that she and her seed will bruise the head of the serpent, and the victory thus remains with our race. Now, to know what is meant by this word *race*, this fruit, or to translate word for word, this blessed seed of the woman, we must listen to Saint Paul on the promise made to Abraham: "By your offspring shall all the nations of the earth bless themselves" (Gen. 22:18). The apostle remarks: "It does not say, 'And to offsprings,' referring to many; but, referring to one, 'And to your offspring,' which is Christ" (Gal. 3:16).

It is thus in him that all the nations shall be blessed, all in one alone. And so in these words addressed to the serpent—"I will put enmity between you and the woman, and between your seed and her seed"—we are to understand that God has in view one son and one fruit; that is, Jesus Christ. And God, who could just as easily have said, and we may think should have said, that he would place this enmity between the dragon and the man, or the fruit of the man, wished instead to say that he would put it between the woman and the fruit of the woman, in order better to point out that this blessed fruit, being born of a virgin, would be the fruit of a woman alone, a woman about whom Saint Elizabeth said, "Blessed are you among women and blessed is the fruit of your womb" (Luke 1:42).

It is you, O Mary, whose fruit will crush the head of the serpent. It is you, O Jesus, who are this blessed fruit in whom our victory is assured. I give you thanks, my God, for having thus brought me hope. And I shall sing to you with David: "O God, thou art my fortress, the God who shows me steadfast love" (Ps. 59:17) and again, "Will the

Lord spurn forever, and never again be favorable? Has God forgotten to be gracious? Has he in anger shut up his compassion?" (Ps. 77:7, 9). No, merciful and good Lord, you were not able — if one dare say it — to hold back your mercy, for on the very day of your anger and at the very pronouncement of the sentence upon our first parents and their entire posterity, your mercy declared itself and you caused the liberator to appear, promising us the victory from that moment.

7

Jesus Christ Promised
to the Patriarchs

The whole human race allowed itself to be corrupted. In the words of Saint Paul: "In past generations [God] allowed all the nations to walk in their own ways" (Acts 14:16). Each people wished to have its own god and to make it according to its fancy. The true God, who had made all things, became the "unknown god" (Acts 17:23) who, although "not far from each one of us" (Acts 17:27) by his works and his gifts, was far removed from our thoughts. A very great evil was triumphing and soon would have become universal. To prevent it, God raised up Abraham, in whom he wished to make a new people and to reunite the peoples of the world in God. That is the sense of these words: "Go from your country and your kindred and your father's house to the land that I will show you. And I will make of you a great nation, and I will bless you, and in you all the families of the earth shall bless themselves" (Gen. 12:1-3). Here then are two things: first, "I will make of you a great nation," which will be the Hebrew people. But my benediction will not end here: I will bless, I will sanctify through you, all the families of the earth, who, participating in your grace as in your faith, will all together be one people that has returned to its Creator after so many centuries.

God alone, his own interpreter, has explained the words: "By you all the families of the earth shall bless themselves," by these, "to your offspring" (Gen. 12:7). That is to say, as the apostle Saint Paul explains both learnedly and devoutly, "and to your offspring" in the singular. There would have to be one fruit, one seed, one son to come forth from Abraham, in whom and by whom would be poured out over all the nations of the earth the benediction promised to them in Abraham. This fruit, this blessed seed, this son of Abraham, was the Christ. This was the very sacred seed promised to the woman at the beginning of our misery, by whom the head of the serpent would be crushed and his empire destroyed.

The same promise was repeated to Isaac and to Jacob. That is why in later days God wished to be known as "the God of Abraham, the God of Isaac, and the God of Jacob" (Exod. 3:6). Yet God sanctifies all the peoples of the earth, not only the Jews who are of the flesh of these patriarchs, but also all the faithful who are the spiritual children of Abraham, who "follow the example of his faith," as Saint Paul puts it (cf. Rom. 4:12). All of this was accomplished only by Jesus Christ, by whom alone the true God, hitherto forgotten by all the peoples of the world, was preached to the Gentiles. Thus were they brought back to him after so many centuries.

This is why all of the prophets point to the calling of the Gentiles as the definitive sign of the Christ, who would come to sanctify all the peoples. And here is that promise made to Abraham, who was thus the founder of our salvation in Christ.

Let us then enter into this divine alliance made with Abraham, Isaac, and Jacob, and let us be true children of the promise. Let us understand the whole power of these words: to be children of the promise is to be the children promised to Abraham. God promised us to this patriarch. If he promised us, then he also gave us. If he promised us, he also made us, for, as the apostle Saint Paul said, "He has the power to accomplish what he has promised" — not to predict, but to accomplish. We are, then, the race that he has made in a particular manner: children of the promise, children of grace, children of the benediction, a new and special people that God has created to serve him. We are not merely to bear his name, but to be a true people, agreeable to God, zealous in good works, and, as children of mercy, chosen and beloved, loving God with all our hearts and our neighbor as ourselves, and extending our love to all nations and all peoples, as to those who are, like us, heirs to his promise. These are the riches hidden in these few words: "In you and in one of your race all the nations of the earth shall be blessed."

8

The Law on Mount Sinai

When God determined to give the law to Moses on Mount Sinai, he did four important things. He descended to the sound of thunder and trumpets. The whole mountain appeared to be on fire, and flames amid a whirlwind of smoke were seen to erupt. God engraved the Decalogue upon two tablets of stone. He pronounced the other articles of the law in a loud and distinct voice, so that all the people could hear.

To publish the law of the gospel, he renewed these four things, but in a still more excellent way. The work began with a great noise, but it was not the violence of thunder, nor the shrill sound of trumpets as is heard amid a battle. The noise that God sent was like the "rush of a mighty wind," and thus an image of the Holy Spirit, which, without being terrifying or menacing, "filled the whole house" (Acts 2:1-2) and called all of Jerusalem to see the beautiful spectacle that God had prepared for it.

"There appeared to them tongues as of fire," but pure and smokeless. These did not appear on the heights in order to frighten the disciples, but the innocent flame rested upon their heads without singeing their hair (Acts 2:3). This fire penetrated within them, and by this means the law of the gospel was impressed upon them mildly, not upon insensible stone, but upon hearts of flesh that had been softened by grace. There was speech, but speech that multiplied itself in the most marvelous way. On Mount Sinai, God had spoken only one language and to one people alone, but the proclamation of the gospel—which was to reunite into one all the peoples of the world in the faith of Jesus Christ and the knowledge of God—was heard in all languages, and "each one heard them speaking in his own language" (Acts 2:6). Thus did Jesus establish his law in a very different way than had Moses. Let us believe, let us hope, let us love, and the law will be in our hearts. Let us prepare for him interior ears, a pure attentiveness, and a filial fear that comes to its perfection in love.

From the heights of Mount Sinai, God cried out: "Take heed that you do not go up into the mountain ... whether beast or man, he shall not live" (Exod. 19:12-13). On the holy mountain of Zion, God not only approaches under the figure of a luminous flame, but he enters within the heart. This beautiful fire takes the shape of a tongue. The Holy Spirit comes to speak to the hearts of the Apostles, and from their hearts will come forth the word that will convert the world.

9

The Prophecy of David

"Blessed is the kingdom of our father David that is coming!" (Mark 11:10). "Hosanna to the son of David!" through whom life and salvation have come to us (Matt. 21:9). The psalms of David are the gospel of Jesus Christ in song, in transports of affection, in thanksgiving, and in holy desires. "This is eternal life, that they know thee the only true God, and Jesus Christ whom thou hast sent" (John 17:3). This is where the psalms begin. The first shows the happiness of the one who keeps the law of God, and then, in the second, Jesus Christ appears. All the powers of the world conspire against him, and God, who laughs at them from on high, addresses his word to Jesus Christ himself, declaring him to be the son that he has begotten from all eternity (Ps. 2:7). From the beginning, this is the argument of all the psalms.

David saw him in the bosom of his father, "from the womb of the morning," that is, before all time, and he saw that he would be his son and at the same time his lord (Ps. 110). David saw that he was a sovereign king, reigning by his beauty, by his graciousness, by his mildness, and by his justice, piercing the heart of his enemies by his just vengeance and the heart of his friends by a holy love. David adored him upon his eternal throne, like a God, whom "your God has anointed" with a holy ointment (Ps. 44), as the father and the protector of the poor, whose name will be honorable before him, as the powerful author of the blessing of the Gentiles (Ps. 70), as the preacher of a new law on the holy mountain of Zion (Ps. 2).

David saw all of the miracles of Christ's life and all of the circumstances of his death; he meditated upon the mystery of it, whole and entire (Ps. 22, 69). In his mind he condemned the disciple who would sell Christ, and he saw his apostolate pass into other hands (Ps. 109).

Christ's pierced hands and feet, his body violently thrown down and crucified, were the dear objects of his tenderness (Ps. 22:16). By his faith, David threw himself into the arms of Christ, stretched out to a people who had rejected him. He tasted the gall and vinegar that Christ was given in his thirst (Ps. 69:21). David saw everything, even the lots cast for his garments that were divided among them (Ps. 22:18). He was touched by the very least circumstances of Christ's death and was unable to forget any of them. He rejoiced in spirit to see Christ, after his death, "proclaim his deliverance to a people yet unborn" (Ps. 22:31), in the great Church, where all the peoples of the world shall be united and where the poor, with the rich, shall be seated at his table. And David followed Christ when he "didst ascend the high mount, leading captives in [his] train" (Ps. 68:18). He adored him, seated at the right hand of the Lord (Ps. 110:5), where Christ was to take his place.

O Jesus, the rare delight, the unique hope, and the love of our father David! This is the reason David was "a man after the Lord's own heart" (1 Sam. 13:14). His tenderness for this dear son, who is the Son of God as well as his own, has gained him the heart of the eternal Father. If he thought so much about the suffering Jesus throughout his life, how much more did he think of him when he became his image in suffering himself. If he was mild to those who offended him; if he was mute, making no reply or defense; if, far from returning evil for evil, he repaid the imprecations of his enemies with prayer; if this good king offered himself to be the victim for his people, who had been laid low by the angel: he saw the example for all these deeds in Jesus. Should we be astonished that he was so humble and so patient in his flight before Absalom? The obedient son consoled him for the

transports and the fury of his own ungrateful and rebellious son.

O Jesus, I come with David to unite myself to your
wounds, to pay homage to you at the throne of your glory,
to submit myself to your power. I rejoice, Son of David,
for all your greatness. No, you have not known corruption (Ps. 16:10), for you are the Holy One of the Lord
(Mark 1:24; cf. Luke 1:35). "Thou dost show me the path
of life; in thy presence there is fullness of joy" (Ps. 16:11).
You "shall reign for ever and ever" and "your kingdom
will have no end" (Rev. 11:15; cf. Luke 1:33).

10

The Conception of John the Baptist

"I am Gabriel, who stand in the presence of God; and I was sent to speak to you, and to bring you this good news" (Luke 1:19). This holy archangel's destiny was a much higher embassy, for he was the one who was to announce the virgin birth. Yet in order that all might be prepared, and to lend credence to the words of his angel, God ordained that he should first announce a birth from a barren woman, and before promising the Christ, God charged him to promise his holy precursor.

One of the characteristics of the works of God is that they are performed at a suitable time; it is one of the most remarkable traits of his wisdom. Zechariah was performing the purest of the priestly duties when the angel of the Lord appeared to him in the Temple. He was offering incense upon the altar set aside for this function, and all the people were outside waiting for him to emerge after he had accomplished the sacred work.

The Conception of John the Baptist

The confusion that came upon him at the sight of the angel was an instance of that religious fear that affects the soul whenever God makes himself present by one means or another. The impression of divine things makes the soul aware of its nothingness; we feel our unworthiness more than ever, and the fear that accompanies the divine disposes us to obedience.

"Do not be afraid," the angel said to him. As the first effect of the divine presence is to cause fear in the depths of the soul, the first effect of the word brought to him from God was to reassure him. "Your prayer is heard, and your wife will bear you a son" (Luke 1:13). He had prayed to God for this gift, and John, like Samuel, was the fruit of prayer. O my soul, pray with faith and perseverance. The angel of the Lord will come, a sweet confidence will follow, a certain heavenly light will appear in your heart, and *John*, that is, grace, will be its fruit. But first we must ask. It is a necessary act of submission that we owe to God; it is the recognition of his power and goodness. The confidence that is the fruit of a pure and faithful love will make itself felt, that is to say, God will make himself felt.

"You shall call his name John" (Luke 1:13). The same angel said to Mary: "You will bear a son, and you shall call his name Jesus" (Luke 1:31). The name *John*, ordained by the angel, is a preparation for a much greater name.

"And you will have joy and gladness, and many will rejoice at his birth" (Luke 1:14). This is the promise of the angel, and this is what we have seen accomplished.

"He will be great before the Lord" (Luke 1:15). The same angel, in announcing Jesus Christ, will repeat the same words, "he will be great," but then add, "and he will be called the Son of the Most High" (Luke 1:32). Jesus will be great like a son; John will be great like a servant, like a herald who marches before his master and inspires respect in all. Jesus is great in his essence, and John will be great by a reflection of the greatness of Jesus. "He shall drink no wine nor strong drink, and he will be filled with the Holy Spirit, even from his mother's womb" (Luke 1:15). Let us recognize in John the character of penance and abstinence. Lord, I recognize him: it is he who will prepare the way for Jesus, and this by penance.

It is also a characteristic of the Nazarene—that is to say, of the saint—to abstain from wine and from all that inebriates. Everything that flatters and transports the senses is an obstacle to holiness. If you avoid drunkenness and the joy of the senses, another drunkenness will be given to you. Like John, you will be filled with the Holy Spirit and transported with celestial joy. Do not allow yourselves to be inebriated by the charms of the senses. Do not allow wine, the joy of the world, to topple your reason. As soon as you taste it, you begin to lose the taste of grace, and you are already troubled. A thick vapor darkens your mind. It is sweet, yes, this is true. Yet it is in this sweetness that it is pernicious. Everything gets jumbled up in our brains, and it is only by chance that we do not fall into some strange disorder. Let us flee, then, let us flee. "Do not look at wine when it is red, when it sparkles in the cup and goes down smoothly, for at last it bites like a serpent, and stings like an adder" (Prov. 23:31-32).

11

The Angelic Salutation

"In the sixth month the angel Gabriel was sent from God to a city of Galilee named Nazareth, to a virgin betrothed to a man whose name was Joseph, of the house of David; and the virgin's name was Mary" (Luke 1:26-27). As soon as we see the angel Gabriel sent forth, we should expect some good news about the coming of the Messiah. It was Gabriel whom God dispatched to Daniel, the man of desires, to tell of the subsequent coming of the Holy of holies who would be anointed and immolated (Dan. 10-11). We have just seen him in his embassy to Zechariah. When we hear the sound of his name again, our desire for Christ should be renewed in heavenly contemplation.

It is neither to Jerusalem, the royal city, nor within the Temple that makes it great, nor in the sanctuary, which is the holiest part of the Temple, nor among the most holy exercises of a wholly divine function, nor to a man as famous for his virtue as for the dignity of his office that the holy angel is sent this time. No, this time God sent Gabriel to a small village in Galilee, one of the least esteemed of the provinces, to the wife of a man who, as she did, truly belonged to the royal household but had been reduced to a humble trade. This was no Elizabeth, whose virtue shone forth due to her husband's rank. It was not thus with the wife of Joseph, who was chosen to be the Mother of Jesus: the wife of an unknown artisan, of a poor carpenter. Ancient tradition teaches us that Mary too earned a living by her work, which is why the most ancient of the Fathers call Jesus Christ the son of a builder and a wage-earner.

This is not the wife of a famous man, whose name was well known: "she had been betrothed to a man named Joseph, and her name was Mary." Concerning externals, then, this second embassy of the angel is much less illustrious than the other. But if we look more deeply, we will discover something much more elevated.

The angel begins with these words of humble greeting: "Hail, Mary, full of grace." Hail, that is, most agreeable to God and full of his gifts, "the Lord is with you, and you are blessed above all women" (cf. Luke 1:28). This discourse is in a much loftier tone than the one that was addressed to Zechariah. To him the angel said, "Do not be afraid," as to a man who has something to fear; and "your prayers have been heard." Yet what is announced to Mary is something so sublime and excellent that she could not have asked for it in her prayers. Mary, humble, hidden, small in his eyes, could not have begun to think that an angel would greet her, especially not with such noble words. It is humility that made her heart troubled. But the angel immediately said, "Do not be afraid, Mary." He did not begin with those words, as we have seen him do with Zechariah, but her humility called forth his reply: "Do not be afraid, Mary, you have found favor with God; you will conceive in your womb and bear a son" (Luke 1:30-31). This miraculous conception will be followed by no less marvelous a birth. There are those who conceive but never give birth, who have only barren, fruitless thoughts. O my God! Grant, O Lord, that following the example of Mary, I too should conceive and give birth. And to whom should I give birth, if not to Jesus Christ? "My little children," said Saint Paul, "I am again in travail until Christ be formed in you!" (Gal. 4:19). As long as Jesus Christ, that is to say, consummate virtue, be not in us, it is only a weak and imperfect conception: Jesus Christ must be born in our souls by true virtues and raised to maturity according to the new law of the gospel.

O Jesus, your reign is eternal: will I ever see it come to an end in my own heart? Will I ever cease to obey you?

The Angelic Salutation

After having begun according to the spirit, will I finish according to the flesh? Will I repent of having done well? Will I hand myself over anew to the tempter, after so many holy efforts to escape from his clutches? Will pride ravage the harvest that is so ready to be gathered in? No, we must be one of those of whom it is written: "Let us not grow weary in well-doing, for in due season we shall reap, if we do not lose heart" (Gal. 6:9).

12

The Virginity of the Mother of God

God, who had predestined the holy Virgin Mary to be associated with the most pure work of our regeneration, inspired in her so great a love of virginity that she not only vowed it, but, even after the angel had declared to her what son she was to conceive, stood ready to refuse the honor of being his mother at the price of her virginity. She thus responded to the angel, "How can this be, because I know not man?" (cf. Luke 1:34) — that is to say, I have resolved for all time not to know one. This resolution is a mark of Mary's exquisite taste for chastity, which made her proof against not only all the promises of man, but also those of God. What could he promise greater than his Son? Yet she is ready to refuse him if it will be necessary to lose her virginity in order to receive him. But God, whose heart is won by this love, has the angel say to her: "The Holy Spirit will come upon you, and the power of the Most High will overshadow you" (Luke

The Virginity of the Mother of God

1:35). God himself will take the place of a spouse; he will unite himself to your body. For this you must be purer than the rays of the sun. The most pure can be united only to purity. He conceives his Son alone in his paternal bosom, not sharing his conception with another, and he does not desire, when the Son is to be born in time, to share it except with a virgin, nor to suffer that he should have two fathers.

Virginity: what is your price! You alone can make a mother of God.

"The Holy Spirit will come upon you, and the power of the Most High will overshadow you; therefore the child to be born will be called holy, the Son of God" (Luke 1:35-56). "Who shall declare his generation?" (cf. Isa. 53:8) It is inexplicable and defies telling. Let us listen nevertheless to what the angel says by the order of God: "The power of the Most High shall overshadow you." The Most High, the heavenly Father, will extend to you his eternal generation. He will produce his Son in your womb and there will make of your blood a body as pure as the Holy Spirit alone can do. At the same time, this divine Spirit will breathe into it a soul, which, having only himself for author, without the cooperation of any other cause, can be nothing other than holy. This soul and this body, by the extension of the generative power of

God, will be united to the person of the Son of God, and henceforth what will be called the Son of God will be this whole composed of the Son of God and man. Therefore "the child to be born will be" properly and truly "called the Son of God." It will also be a holy thing by its nature. Holy, not with a derived and accidental holiness, but substantively—the Holy—something fitting only to God, who is holy according to his nature. The Word and the Son of God will be personally united to the body formed of your blood, and to its soul, according to the eternal laws imposed upon all of nature by its Creator. This being, this divine composite, will be altogether the Son of God and your own.

Here then is a new created dignity upon the earth, the dignity of the Mother of God, which includes graces so great that thought must not attempt or even hope to understand them. The perfect virginity of body and soul is a part of this high dignity. For if concupiscence, which since the Fall ordinarily attaches to the conception of men, had been found in this one, then Jesus Christ would have contracted the primitive stain, he, the one who came to efface it. It was, therefore, necessary that Jesus Christ be the son of a virgin, and that he be conceived by the Holy Spirit. Thus also Mary remained a virgin and became a mother.

The Virginity of the Mother of God

Chaste mysteries of Christianity, how pure must we be to understand them! Yet how much more pure must we be to express them in our lives by the sincere practice of Christian truth! We no longer belong to the earth, we whose faith is so exalted; "our commonwealth is in heaven" (Phil. 3:20).

13

The Handmaiden of the Lord

The angel continued: "And behold, your kinswoman Elizabeth in her old age has also conceived a son; and this is the sixth month with her who was called barren. For with God nothing will be impossible" (Luke 1:36-37). Mary did not need to be presented with examples of divine omnipotence. It was for us, to whom the mystery of her Annunciation would be revealed, that the angel spoke these words.

Mary was transported in her admiration of the divine power in all its degrees. She saw that, in the frequently repeated miracle of making the barren to be fruitful, God had desired to prepare the world for the unique and new miracle of a child born of a virgin, and transported in spirit with a holy joy by the miracle that God wished to work in her, she said with a submissive voice, "Behold, I am the handmaiden of the Lord; let it be to me according to your word" (Luke 1:38).

The Handmaiden of the Lord

God did not need the consent and the obedience of the holy Virgin to do with her what he willed or even to have Jesus Christ be born of her, and to form in her womb the body that he wished to unite with the person of his Son, but he wanted to give great examples to the world and the great mystery of the Incarnation to be accompanied by every sort of virtue in all those who had any part in it. This is the reason the virtues that the Gospel invites us to admire were placed in the holy Virgin and in her chaste spouse, Saint Joseph.

Here is an even loftier mystery. The disobedience of our mother Eve, her incredulity toward God, and her miserable credulity toward the deceitful angel had entered into the work of our loss, and God desired also that the obedience of Mary and her humble faith would enter into the work of our redemption. In this way our nature was repaired in everything that had entered into its loss, and so that we would have a new Eve in Mary, just as we have a new Adam in Jesus Christ, so that we might be able to say to this virgin, with holy sighs: We cry out to you, poor, banished children of Eve, mourning and weeping in this valley of tears: offer them to your dear Son, and show us at our end the blessed fruit of your womb that you have received in this way.

This is the solid foundation for the great devotion that the Church has always had for the Blessed Virgin. She has the same part in our salvation that Eve had in our loss. It is a doctrine that has been received throughout the entire Catholic Church in a tradition that stretches back to the very origin of Christianity. It will unfold in all of the mysteries of the Gospel. Let us enter into the profundity of this plan; let us imitate the obedience of Mary, for it is by her that the human race has been saved and, according to the ancient promise, that the head of the serpent has been crushed.

14

The Three Virtues
of the Annunciation

Holy virginity had to be the first disposition of the Mother of God, for a purity that transcended that of the angels was necessary in order for her to be united to the eternal Father and to bear the Son. This disposition prepared her to be overshadowed by the power from on high and visited by the Holy Spirit. The lofty resolution to renounce forever all joys of the senses, as if one were without a body, is what makes a virgin and what prepared an earthly mother for the Son of God.

Yet all this would have been nothing without humility. The fallen angels were chaste, but for all their chastity, God consigned them to hell because they were proud. It was, therefore, necessary that Mary be humble to the same extent that these rebels had been proud. This is why she said, "I am the handmaiden of the Lord." Nothing less would have sufficed to make her Christ's mother. But the last disposition was faith. For she must conceive the Son of God in her spirit before conceiving him in her body, and this was the work of faith alone: "Let it be to me according to thy word." From that moment the word entered into the Blessed Virgin like a celestial sowing; as she received it, so she conceived the Word in her spirit.

Let us then have a firm faith, and let us hope for everything from the divine goodness and the divine promises. The Word will become incarnate in us. We will participate in the dignity of the Mother of God, in accord with Christ's teaching: "My mother and my brethren are those who hear the word of God and do it" (Luke 8:21).

15

In the Beginning Was the Word

Can Jesus Christ, as he was before all ages, be an object of our knowledge? He can, for it is to us that the Gospel has been addressed. Let us follow the eagle of the Evangelists, the beloved among the disciples, another John than John the Baptist. Let us follow John the Son of Thunder, who does not speak a human language, but who lights up, who booms, who deafens. John brings every created mind to the obedience of faith, when by a rapid flight, cutting through the air, piercing the clouds, raising himself above the angels, the virtues, the cherubim and seraphim, he intones his Gospel with these words: "*In the beginning was the Word*" (John 1:1). It is here that he begins to make Jesus Christ known. We must go further back than the Annunciation of Mary.

Let us consider well: *in the beginning was the Word*. Why say the *beginning* when speaking of the one who had no beginning? It is in order to say that at the beginning, at the origin of things, *he was*. He did not begin: *he was*. He was not created, he was not made: *he was*. And what was he? What was the one who, without having been made and without having a beginning, already was when God began everything? Was it a mixture of matter upon which God set himself to work, to change and to form? No. What was at the beginning *was the Word*, the interior word, thought, reason, intelligence, wisdom, the interior discourse, *sermo*, a discourse without running over, that is, not a discourse from which one derives one thing from another by reasoning, but a discourse in which every truth exists substantially, and which is the truth itself.

Where am I? What do I see? What do I hear? Be silent, reason. And without reasoning, without speech, without images drawn from the senses, without words formed by the tongue, without the help of vibrating air, or an imagination that has been stirred, without anxiety or human effort, let us say within ourselves, let us say by faith and with a captive and submissive understanding: *in the beginning*, without beginning, before every beginning, above every beginning, *was* the one who is and who endures forever, *the Word*, the eternal and substantial thought of God.

He was, he was subsistent, but not as something separated from God, for *he was in God* (cf. John 1:1). And how shall we explain *to be in God*? Was he in God in the manner of an accident, as our individual thoughts happen to be in us? No. The Word is not in God in that way. But how then? How shall we explain what has been said to us by our eagle, by our evangelist? "The Word was with God: *apud Deum*" (John 1:1). This was to say that he was not something inhering in God, or something that affected God, but something that remained in him as subsisting in him, as being a person in God, and another person than this God in whom he is. And this person is a divine person: *and the Word was God*. How? Was he God without a source? No, because this God is the Son of God, the only Son, as Saint John will soon call him. "We have," he said, "beheld his glory, glory as of the only Son from the Father" (John 1:14).

This Word, then, is in God, remains in God, subsists in God, is in God a person processing from God himself and remaining in him, always produced, always in his bosom: *unigenitus Filius qui est in sinu Patris* — "the only-begotten Son who is in the bosom of the Father" (cf. John 1:18). He is produced there, inasmuch as he is Son; he remains there because he is the eternally subsisting thought. He is God like him, for the Word was God. God in God, God from God, begotten by God, subsisting in God, God, like him, "over all things ... blessed for ever. Amen," in the words of Saint Paul (Rom. 9:5).

Ah! I am lost. I can go no further. I can but say, "Amen, it is thus." What silence. What wonder. What astonishment. What new light. But what ignorance. I see nothing, and I see all. I see this God who was at the beginning, who is in the bosom of the Father, and I do not see him. "Amen, it is thus." This is all that remains of the whole discourse that I have just made, a simple and irrevocable acquiescence, through love, in the truth that my faith shows to me. Amen, amen, amen. And once more, amen. And forever, amen.

16

All Things Were
Made Through Him

In the beginning, the Word subsisted in God. Ascend to
the beginning of all things; push your thoughts as far as
you can. Go to the beginning of the human race. He was.
Go to the first day, when God said "Let there be light."
He was. Continue to ascend. Rise higher than the days
before the first day, when everything was chaos and darkness. He was. When the angels were created in the truth,
in which Satan and his minions did not remain, he was.
In the beginning, before everything that had a beginning,
he was. He was alone, in his Father, beside his Father, in
the bosom of his Father. He was, and what was he? Who
will be able to say? Who will recount for us, who will explain his generation? (Isa. 53:8). He *was*; like his Father,
he is the one who is (Exod. 3:14). He is the perfect one;
he is the existent one, the subsistent one, being itself. But
what was he? Who knows? We know nothing other than

that he was, that is to say, he was, but he was begotten by God, subsistent in God; that is, he was God and he was Son.

Where do we see that he was? "All things were made through him, and without him was not anything made that was made" (John 1:3). Let us, if we can, conceive of the difference between the one who was and everything that was made. To be the one who was, and through whom all things were made, and to be made: what an immense distance separates these two things! To be and to make, this is what is proper to the Word. To be made, this is what is proper to the Creature. He was, therefore, as one by whom all that was made was to have been made. What force, what distinctness to express clearly that all was made by the Word: all through him, nothing without him. What remains in human language to signify that the Word was the Creator of all, or, what is the same thing, that God is the Creator of all through the Word? For he is the Creator of all, not by any effort, but by simple commandment, as it is written in the book of Genesis, and similarly in this verse of David: "For he spoke, and it came to be; he commanded, and it stood forth" (Ps. 33:9).

We must not understand this *through* to refer to anything material or ministerial. All things were made through the Word, just as every intelligent being makes what he makes by his reason, by his thought, by his wisdom. This is why, if it is said here that God made everything through his Word, which is his wisdom and his thought, it is said elsewhere that "the eternal Wisdom that he had begotten in his bosom, and that he had conceived and given birth to before the hills, is with him, together with him ordered and arranged all things, rejoiced in his presence, and delighted himself by the facility and variety of his designs and his works" (cf. Prov. 8:22-31). And accordingly it was said to Moses that "God saw all that he had made" by his command, which is his Word, and that he was pleased, "and saw that it was good, and very good" (Gen. 1:18, 21, 25, 31). Where did he see this goodness of the things that he had made, if it was not in the very goodness of the wisdom and of the thought by which he had destined and ordered them? This is also why he said "he had possessed," that is to say, that he had begotten, he had conceived, he had given birth to his wisdom, in which he had seen and ordered the beginning of his ways (Prov. 8:22). He delighted in his wisdom, and this eternal Wisdom, full of goodness and infinitely beneficent, found its pleasure and delight in being and in living with men, a delight brought to fulfillment when the Word was made man, "was made flesh," was incarnate, and "dwelt among us" (John 1:14).

Let us also delight in the Word, in the thought, in the wisdom of God. Let us listen to the speech of the one who talks to us in a profound and wonderful silence. Let us lend him the ear of our heart. Let us say to him, like Samuel: "Speak, Lord, for thy servant hears" (1 Sam. 3:10). Let us love prayer, which is communication with and familiarity with God. Who will impose silence upon himself and upon all that is not God, and let his heart flow peaceably toward the Word, toward the eternal Wisdom, especially now that he has "been made man" and has "dwelt among us"? Among us, *in nobis,* in what is most intimately ours, according to what has been written: "He found out all the way of knowledge, and gave it to Jacob his servant, and to Israel his beloved. Afterward he was seen upon earth, and conversed with men" (cf. Bar. 3:36-37).

What virtues should be born in us from this commerce with God and with his Word! What humility! What self-abnegation! What devotion! What love of truth! What generosity! What candor! May our speech be straightforward and plain—may our yes be yes and our no be no—and may we be truthful in all things, for the truth "abides with us" (cf. 1 John 4:12).

17

Life and Light in the Word

"In him was life, and the life was the light of men" (John 1:4). By saying that there is life in plants, we mean that they grow and send forth leaves, buds, and fruit. How crude is this life, and how dead. We say that animals live because they see, taste, and go here and there as they are moved by their senses. How mute is this life. We also say that life is to understand, to know, to know oneself, to know God and to desire him, to love him, and to wish to be happy in him. This is the true life. Yet what is its source? Who is it that knows himself, loves himself, and enjoys himself, unless it is the Word? In him, therefore, is life. Yet whence does it come, if not from his eternal and living generation? He is come forth alive from a Father who is alive, about whom he himself pronounced: "As the Father has life in himself, so also he has granted to the Son to have life in himself" (John 5:26). He did not give him life as drawn forth from nothingness; he gave him life from his own life and proper substance, and as he is the source of life, he has given his Son to be a source of life. And so this life of understanding is "the light that enlightens every man" (John 1:9). From the life and light of the Word come forth all understanding and light.

This light of life shone in heaven, in the splendor of the saints, on the mountains, on exalted spirits, on the angels, but it also wished to shine among men, who had withdrawn from it. The light came near to them and, in order to enlighten them, set a torch before their very eyes by preaching the gospel. So it was that "the light shines in the darkness, and the darkness did not comprehend it" (cf. John 1:5). "The people who sat in darkness have seen a great light, and for those who sat in the region and shadow of death, light has dawned" (Matt. 4:16).

The light shines in the darkness, and the darkness did not comprehend it. Proud souls have not understood the humility of Jesus Christ. Souls blinded by their passions have not understood Jesus Christ, who intended nothing but the will of his Father. Curious souls, who wish to see for the pleasure of it and not to rule their habits and mortify their concupiscence, have understood nothing of Jesus Christ, who began by doing and then afterward taught (cf. Acts 1:1). They were miserable, those mortals who "wished to rejoice in his light" but not to let their hearts be embraced by "the fire" that Jesus Christ had come to ignite (John 5:35; Luke 12:49). Those with pre-occupied souls, entirely withdrawn into themselves, have not understood Jesus Christ, nor the heavenly precept of self-renunciation. The light is come, and the darkness did not comprehend it. But what of the light? Did the light comprehend the light? Those who said "we see" (cf. John 9:41) and who blinded themselves by their presumption: have they better comprehended Jesus Christ? No, the priests did not comprehend him. The Pharisees did not comprehend him. The doctors of the law did not comprehend him. Jesus Christ was an enigma to them. They could not suffer the truth, for it humiliated, corrected, and condemned them. And they in their turn humiliated, tormented, contradicted, and crucified truth itself.

Do we comprehend it, we who call ourselves his disciples, but who nonetheless wish to please men and ourselves? Let us humble ourselves and say: the light still shines in the darkness every day by faith and the gospel, but the darkness has not comprehended it, and Jesus Christ finds hardly anyone willing to imitate him.

"The true light that enlightens every man was coming into the world" and dwelt among us, but without having been noticed. "He was in the world," the one who was the light, "and the world was made through him, yet the world knew him not. He came into his own home, and his own people received him not" (John 1:9-11). His own people did not receive him, but, in another sense, his own people did receive him. Those who were touched by a certain instinct of grace did receive him. The sinners whom he called left everything to follow him. A tax collector followed him at his first word. All the humble followed him, and these were truly his own people. The proud, the falsely wise, the Pharisees were also his people, for he had made them, and he had made this faithless world that did not wish to know him.

O Jesus! I would be like them if you had not converted me. Complete the work. Pull me away from the world that you have made, but whose corruption you did not make. Everything in it is curiosity, greed, the concupiscence of the eyes, impurity, the concupiscence of the flesh, and the pride of life, a pride with which all of life is infected (1 John 2:16). O Jesus! Send to me one of your heavenly fishermen who will pull me out of this sea of corruption and catch me in the net of your word.

18

And the Word Was Made Flesh

"To all who received him, who believe in his name, he gave power to become children of God" (John 1:12). To believe in the name of Jesus Christ is to recognize him as the Christ, as the Son of God, as the Word who was before all time and who became man. To be ready at the sound of that name, and for the glory of that name alone, to do all things, to attempt all things, to suffer all things: this is what it means to believe in the name of Jesus Christ.

They are born not "of blood, nor of the will of the flesh, nor of the will of man, but of God" (John 1:13). God has given us the freedom to choose to become his children and to cooperate in our generation by faith. This power nevertheless comes from God, who places in us the divine seed of his word, not one that strikes the ears, but one that finds a secret path into our hearts.

And what is the source of this great gift? "And the Word was made flesh, and dwelt among us, full of grace and truth; we have beheld his glory, glory as of the only Son from the Father" (John 1:14). To make us children of God, it was necessary that his only Son become a man. It must be through this unique and essential Son that we receive the spirit of adoption. The Son has come to us, and we have seen his glory. He was the light, and it is by the brilliance and in the reflection of this light that we have been regenerated. He was the "true light that enlightens every man"; he enlightens the children that come into the world, giving them their reason, which, obscured as it is, is nevertheless a light and will develop with time.

Yet another light by which he still comes to enlighten the world is his Gospel, which he continually offers to the whole world, even to the little children who are enlightened by Baptism. And when he regenerates us and makes us children of God, what does he do but cause his light to be born in our hearts, a light by which we see him, full of grace and truth—full of grace from his miracles and truth from his words. "For it is the God who said, 'Let light shine out of darkness,' who has shone in our hearts to give the light of the knowledge of the glory of God in the face of Christ" (2 Cor. 4:6). We are thus children of God because we are children of the light. Let us walk as children of the light. Let us not desire vain glory or the deceitful pomp of human grandeur. All of it is false; all of it is darkness. The world that wishes to lure us has no grace at all. Jesus Christ alone, full of grace and truth, knows how to fill our hearts, and he alone should attract us. Grace is poured out upon his lips and upon his speech (cf. Ps. 45:2; Luke 4:22). Everything in him is pleasing, even his Cross, where we see shining forth his obedience, his generosity, his grace, his redemption, his salvation. All the rest is less than nothing. Jesus Christ alone is full of grace and truth. It is for us that he is full, and "from his fullness we have all received, grace upon grace" (John 1:16).

19

Jesus the Christ,
the Anointed One

O Christ! O Messiah! You whom we hoped for and who were given to us with this sacred name signifying the anointed one of the Lord: help us to see the origins of Christianity in the excellence of your anointing. It is written that "the anointing will teach you all things," and again, "we have the anointing" and "we know all things" (cf. 1 John 2:20, 27). What does it teach us unless it is that the anointing that made you the Christ also made us Christians by the communication of so lovely a name?

O Christ! You are known from all time according to this beautiful name. When the psalmist saw you, he heard this name, for he sang, "Your throne, O God, is eternal, and your God has anointed you with oil" (cf. Ps. 45:6-7). It is you that Solomon praised, saying in his divine canticle: "Your name is an oil, a balm that is poured out" (cf. Song of Sol. 1:3). When the angel Saint Gabriel announced the time of your coming, he explained himself by saying that "the Holy of holies will be anointed" and that "the Anointed One," that is, the Christ, "will be sacrificed" (Dan. 9:21-26). And what did you yourself preach in the synagogue when you explained your mission? What did you preach but that beautiful text of Isaiah: "The Spirit of the Lord has sent me, and it is for this that he anointed me"? (cf. Isa. 61:1; Luke 4:18).

Jesus is anointed by the Holy Spirit, not by the material oil that anointed Aaron and the priests, Elijah and the prophets, David and the kings. Although priest, prophet, and king, Jesus was not anointed with this anointing; indeed, it was but the shadow of his own. Thus, David said that "he was anointed with an excellent oil, above all those that are said to be anointed" (cf. Ps. 45:7). What David points to is the anointing with divinity and the Holy Spirit, by which God made him the Christ. And with the same Spirit he filled his newborn Church and spread the name *Christian* throughout the whole world. Yet we must not stop with the acknowledgment of this doctrine—although it is divine and necessary—we must apply it in the way that God commands us to.

By his anointing, Jesus Christ is priest, prophet, and king. It is in this way that he is the Christ, and it is in the same manner that we are Christians. For, by the generous outpouring of his anointing, we are made kings and we are able to offer sacrifice, "a royal priesthood," as Saint Peter says (1 Pet. 2:9). And as Saint John says in the book of Revelation: "Jesus Christ has made us kings and the priests of God his Father" (cf. Rev. 1:6).

We must then have a truly royal courage, not allowing ourselves to be subjected in any way to our passions. We must have only the loftiest of thoughts, not allowing ourselves to be enslaved by earthly ones.

As kings, let us be magnanimous and tremendously generous. Let us aspire to the noblest deeds, but let us aspire to them as priests who offer spiritual sacrifices to the Most Holy. Christians, we are no longer men of the world; we are those to whom it has been said, "You shall be holy, for I am holy" (1 Pet. 1:16).

In what way are we prophets? Let us act by a heavenly instinct. Let us leave the walls of this present world, and let us be filled with the things that are to come. We should breathe only eternity. But you are making a home for yourself upon the earth. You wish to rise in stature here. Dream instead of a land in which you shall be a king: "Fear not, little flock, for it is your Father's good pleasure to give you the kingdom" (Luke 12:32).

20

The Virtues of the Anointing of a Christian

One of the principal effects of the Christian faith and of the holy anointing of the children of God is gentleness. "Learn from me," said Jesus himself, "for I am gentle and lowly in heart" (Matt. 11:29). Isaiah predicted his gentleness in these words that Saint Matthew later applied to Christ: "Behold my servant, whom I uphold, my chosen, in whom my soul delights; I have put my Spirit upon him, he will bring forth justice to the nations." Here is a most extraordinary servant, who "will not cry or lift up his voice," as the contentious and the disputatious do. How gentle he is, and how humble! "A bruised reed he will not break, and a dimly burning wick he will not quench" (Isa. 42:1, 3; cf. Matt. 12:18-19). Here is the spirit of Jesus Christ and the true spirit of God, which was not in the "great and strong wind" that "rent the mountains," as Elijah, wishing him to exterminate and destroy all things, seemed to think; nor was he in the earthquake or the fire, but instead in the gentle breeze, in the light and refreshing air of the "still small voice" (1 Kings 19:11-12).

Such is the spirit of the Lord Jesus. This is why, when his disciples wished—in the spirit of Elijah and Elisha—to call down fire from heaven upon the villages that refused to welcome them, he said to them in his ineffable gentleness, "You do not know what manner of spirit you are of" (Luke 9:55). This was to say: "You do not know the spirit of your religion and of the doctrine of Christ." Such was his gentleness that he said to those who struck him: "If I have spoken wrongly, bear witness to the wrong; but if I have spoken rightly, why do you strike me?" (John 18:23). And elsewhere: "O faithless generation, how long am I to be with you? How long am I to bear with you? Bring him to me" that I may heal him (Mark 9:19; Luke 9:41). And again: "Woman, where are they? Has no one condemned you? Neither do I condemn you" (John 8:10-11).

Let us then put on a spirit of gentleness, the true spirit of the Christian faith. May the anointing of the Holy Spirit sweeten our bitterness and soften our pride. Let not our speech be haughty and disdainful, for it is weakness that causes us to act that way. Strength lies in calm reasoning, and is absent when one is reduced to contentiousness in order to support a bad argument. When you must fight for the truth, consider that it was not at all by bitter disputes that the gospel was established, but by gentleness and patience, by imitating Jesus Christ, who was "like a sheep that before its shearers is dumb" (Isa. 53:7) and who even let himself be scourged without complaining. Listen to the preachers of his gospel when they were condemned by the Jews: "Whether it is right in the sight of God to listen to you rather than to God, you must judge; for we cannot but speak of what we have seen and heard" (Acts 4:19-20). It is in this spirit that one must speak to those whom the truth obliges us to oppose. It is in this way — without disputatiousness or vexation — that they are shown to be in the wrong. These are the actions of true Christians and true imitators of Christ.

Let us again listen to the same part of the Acts of the Apostles and hear the innocent flock so unjustly mistreated: "Sovereign Lord, who didst make the heaven and the earth, look upon their threats, and grant to thy servants to speak thy word with all boldness, while thou stretchest out thy hand to heal, and signs and wonders are performed through the name of thy holy servant Jesus" (Acts 4:24, 29-30). Thus they spoke with confidence and without either discouragement or bitterness. He who places his confidence in God does not place it in the violence of a bitter and imperious tone. Victory belongs to gentleness and patience; and Isaiah, having shown Jesus Christ to be so humble, so patient, and so gentle, concludes by saying: "He will not fail or be discouraged till he brings justice to victory, and in his name will the Gentiles hope" (cf. Isa. 42:4; Matt. 12:20-21). So you must go about God's business with gentleness. Be true Christians, that is to say, true lambs, and without murmur, without noise, without any tincture of the spirit of contradiction, show as much tranquillity as you do innocence. Lay hold of gentleness and of patience her daughter: these two virtues are the proper characteristics of Christian piety and the fruits of the anointing of Jesus Christ poured out upon us.

21

The Oblation of Jesus Christ

"He has appeared . . . to put away sin by the sacrifice of himself," said Saint Paul (Heb. 9:26). It is his very self, his own body and blood, that he has offered on the Cross. It is still his own body and blood that he offers in the daily sacrifice. It is not, then, without reason that David, seeing in the Spirit the first act that Jesus Christ would accomplish in making himself man, said: "Burnt offering and sin offering thou hast not required. Then I said, 'Lo, I come; in the roll of the book it is written of me; I delight to do your will, O my God' " (Ps. 40:6-8). Interpreting this prophecy, Saint Paul added: "Sacrifices and offerings thou has not desired, but a body has thou prepared for me" (Heb. 10:5). By these words, Jesus Christ places himself at the head of all the ancient victims; and because there was nothing in his divinity that he could sacrifice to God, God gave him a body suitable for suffering and proportioned to the condition of victim in which he placed himself.

Once he had begun this great action, he never ceased, and he remained from his infancy, and even in his mother's womb, in the condition of victim, abandoned to the commands of God, to suffer and to do what he willed.

"I come to do thy will, as it is written at the beginning of your book: *in capite libri.*" There is an eternal book in which is written what God wills for all his elect, and at the head of it, what he wills in particular for Jesus Christ, who is the head of the elect. The first article of this book is that Jesus Christ will take the place of every victim by doing the will of God with perfect obedience. It is to God's will that he submits himself, which is why David added, "I delight to do your will, O my God; thy law is written within my heart" (Ps. 40:8).

Let us then follow the example of Jesus Christ with the spirit of a victim who is abandoned to the will of God—otherwise we will have no part in his sacrifice. It was necessary for him to be a burnt offering and a victim entirely consumed by fire; we ought to allow ourselves to be reduced to ashes rather than to oppose God's desires.

It is in the holy will of God that equanimity and repose are to be found. In the life of the passions and of self-rule, we think of one thing today and another tomorrow, one thing during the night and another during the day, one thing when we are sad and another when seized by a good mood, one thing when hope smiles upon our desires and another when it withdraws from us. The only remedy for these vagaries and inconsistencies in our lives is complete submission to the will of God. As God is always the same amid all the changes he brings about in his creation, so the man submitted to his will is always the same. For reason to be sovereign is what God wants. The will of God, entirely holy, is itself our reason.

Let us nevertheless take care that it be not through laziness or a kind of despair, and to give ourselves a false repose, that we have recourse to the will of God. The divine will gives us repose through our own actions and when we do what is required of us. It brings us repose in sorrow as well as in joy, according to the pleasure of the one who knows what is good for us. It brings us repose not in self-satisfaction, but in contentment with God, as we pray to him to be pleased with us and to do with us what he wills. What does it matter what becomes of us upon the earth? There is but one thing to ask of the Lord: "that I may dwell in the house of the Lord all the days of my life, to behold the beauty of the Lord, and to inquire in his temple" (Ps. 27:4).

Let us begin that life by singing with David, or rather with Jesus Christ, the hymn of the holy will: "Here I am, Lord, I come to do your will."

22

Mary Goes to Visit Elizabeth

As soon as Mary had conceived the Word in her womb, she "arose and went with haste to the hill country, to a city of Judah" (Luke 1:39) to visit her cousin Elizabeth. Can we not sense the cause of this promptness, of the seriousness with which she took this duty? When one is filled with Jesus Christ, one is at the same time filled with charity, with a holy vivacity, and with lofty ideals, whose execution leaves no time for languishing. Mary, who carried grace with Jesus Christ in her womb, was called forth by a divine instinct to take that grace to the house of Zechariah, where John the Baptist had been recently conceived.

It is for superiors to abase themselves and to serve. Mary, knowing herself to have been served by the Word who had descended into her womb, could not fail to be touched by the desire to humble herself and to abase herself according to his example. Jesus would need to be

Mary Goes to Visit Elizabeth

preceded by Saint John externally, but interiorly, it is Jesus who must precede, because he must sanctify John. It was necessary that John receive from Jesus the first touch of grace.

In all of the visits that we make, let us imitate Mary. Let us visit one another in charity, for under even a simple civility great mysteries may be hidden. Grace will grow where it is made known by humility and by the exercise of holy friendship.

Pious souls, cultivate the duties of family life. Be friends, Christian women, as Mary and Elizabeth were. Let your friendship be a work of piety and your conversations full of God; then Jesus will be in your midst and you will feel his presence.

Men, you too should imitate these pious women. O God! Sanctify our conversations, remove from them curiosity, dissipation, anxiety, dissimulation, and trickery. Allow cordiality and good examples to reign in them.

For this day is a miracle! Jesus Christ is hidden, and yet he is the one who accomplishes everything. Neither movement nor sound comes forth from him, yet he causes the infant in Elizabeth's womb to move. Jesus, who is the mover of all things, is the only one here who seems to be without an action; his action is apparent only in those he inspires in the others.

We see here three persons whom Jesus Christ works upon, three different dispositions of the souls he approaches. "Why is this granted me?" says Elizabeth (Luke 1:43). She is astonished at the approach of God; not being able to discover the reason for it in her own merit, she is astounded by God's goodness. In other souls, God works the motion and the holy effort to make them come to him: this is what is apparent in the leaping of John the Baptist. His last work is peace in the glorification of the divine power; and this is what is apparent in the Blessed Virgin. Let us then see in these three persons moved in three different ways, the three divine operations of Jesus Christ in Christian souls: in Elizabeth, the humble astonishment of a soul he approaches; in John the Baptist, the holy transport of a soul he draws toward himself; and in Mary, the ineffable peace of a soul he possesses.

23

The Humble
Astonishment of Elizabeth

At Mary's voice and her words of greeting, "the babe leaped in her womb, and Elizabeth was filled with the Holy Spirit, and she exclaimed with a loud cry [this loud cry expressed at once both surprise and joy]: "Blessed are you among women, and blessed is the fruit of your womb!" (Luke 1:41-42). The one whom you carry is the one in whom all nations shall be blessed; he has begun by pouring out his benediction upon you. "And why is this granted me, that the mother of my Lord should come to me?" (Luke 1:43). Souls who are astonished to meet God, because his presence was unlooked for, first attempt to draw back as being unworthy of the grace. "Depart from me, Lord," said Saint Peter, "for I am a sinful man" (cf. Luke 5:8). Likewise, the Centurion: "Lord, I am not worthy to have you come under my roof" (Matt. 8:8). In a similar sentiment, but milder, Elizabeth, even though confirmed in virtue, is surprised to see herself approached by the Lord in so admirable a manner. "Why is this granted me, that the mother of my Lord," and the one who carries him in her womb, "should come to me?" She senses that it is the Lord who comes himself, but that he comes and he acts by his holy Mother. "For behold," she said, "when the voice of your greeting came to my ears, the babe in my womb leaped for joy" (Luke 1:44). He senses the presence of the master and begins to fulfill the office of the precursor, not yet by his voice, but by this sudden leap. Even his voice was not absent, inasmuch as he had secretly inspired his mother's. Jesus came to him through his Mother, and John recognized him through his own.

In this dispensation of graces by Jesus Christ to Saint Elizabeth and her son at the visitation of the holy Virgin, the advantage is entirely on the side of the child. Accordingly, one of the holy Fathers said: "Elizabeth was the first to hear the voice, but John was the first to be sensible of the grace. Elizabeth," continued Saint Ambrose, "had been the first to perceive Mary's arrival, but John the first to be sensible of the arrival of Jesus."

Elizabeth, recovering from her astonishment, proceeds further in her praise of the holy Virgin. "Blessed is she who believed that there would be a fulfillment of what

The Humble Astonishment of Elizabeth

was spoken to her from the Lord" (Luke 1:45). You have conceived as a virgin, and you will give birth as a virgin; your Son will succeed to the throne of David, and his reign will have no end.

Let us then believe, and we too will be blessed like Mary. Let us believe like her in the reign of Jesus and in the promises of God. Let us say with faith: "Thy kingdom come." Let us cry out with all the people: "Blessed is he who comes in the name of the Lord! Blessed is the kingdom of our father David" (Mark 11:9-10).

Blessedness is attached to faith. You are blessed to have believed. "Blessed are you, Simon ... for flesh and blood has not revealed to you" this faith that you have pronounced, "but my Father who is in heaven" (Matt. 16:17). Whence this blessedness of faith? "Blessed is she who believed that there would be a fulfillment of what was spoken to her" (Luke 1:45). You have believed; you will see. You were faithful to the promises; you will receive the reward. You have sought God in faith; you will find him in joy.

Let us then place all of our happiness in faith. Let us not be insensible to this beatitude. It is Jesus Christ himself who offers it to us, and the glory of God and his will are found in our blessedness. The one who is blessed is at the same time excellent. One is blessed to believe; there is nothing either more excellent or better than faith, which, founded upon the divine promise, abandons itself to the will of God and thinks only of how to please him.

24

My Soul Magnifies the Lord

The initial transports of a soul taken out of itself and no longer knowing itself are followed by an ineffable calm, a peace surpassing all the senses, and a celestial hymn.

"My soul magnifies the Lord, and my spirit rejoices in God my Savior" (Luke 1:46). What is to be said about this divine canticle? Its simplicity and loftiness rise above our intellect and invite us to silence rather than to speech. God himself must teach us what to think of it. Here we meet a soul who has left herself behind completely and glories only in God, finding all her joy in him; she is at peace, for nothing can take away the one of whom she sings.

"My soul magnifies, my soul exalts the Lord." After she has exhausted herself celebrating his greatness, no matter how lofty her contemplation, she exalts him still more, rising higher and higher, above all things, until she is lost from view. "My spirit rejoices in God my Savior."

At the very name of *Savior*, my senses rejoice, and I find in him the salvation I cannot find in myself.

"For he has looked upon the lowliness of his servant" (cf. Luke 1:48). If I were to think that it depended upon me to attract his regard, my lowliness and nothingness would deprive me of all hope and rest. Yet because he has looked upon me voluntarily and from pure goodness, I have an imperishable support in the mercy with which he has regarded me, for he is kind and generous.

She declares her blessings, whose source she knows to be God and which can come only from God. "And behold," she says, "all generations shall call me blessed" (Luke 1:48). Having thus been raised to the highest contemplation, she begins to join her happiness to that of all redeemed peoples in the second part of her song.

"For he who is mighty has done great things for me, and holy is his name. And his mercy is on those who fear him from generation to generation" (Luke 1:49-50). She sees that her happiness is the happiness of all the earth, and that she is carrying the one in whom all nations shall be blessed. She considers the holiness and the power of God, who is the cause of these wonders.

The one who alone is powerful has accomplished in me a work worthy of his power alone: the God-man, stripped of all possessions yet Savior of the world, conqueror of the virtuous and victor over the proud. "And holy is his name." God is holiness itself. He is holy, and he makes things to be holy. When does he appear more holy but when his Son is also Mary's, and when he pours out mercy, grace, and holiness from generation to generation upon those who fear him?

If we wish to partake of this grace, let us be holy, and we will proclaim with all the nations that Mary is blessed.

25

He Has Put Down the Mighty
from Their Thrones

Mary spoke further of God's power so as to explain the
effects of the Incarnation of the Son of God. "He has
shown strength with his arm, he has scattered the proud
in the imagination of their hearts, he has put down the
mighty from their thrones, and exalted those of low de-
gree" (Luke 1:51-52). When did he accomplish all these
wonders if it was not when he sent into the world his
Son, who has confounded kings and proud empires by
the preaching of his gospel? In this work his power shone
forth all the more because "God chose what is weak in
the world to shame the strong ... even things that are
not, to bring to nothing things that are, so that no human being might boast in the presence of God" (1 Cor.
1:27-29), and so that everything might be attributed to
the power of his arm alone. This is why he abased himself
in our midst. And when he said, "I thank thee, Father,

He Has Put Down the Mighty

Lord of heaven and earth, that thou hast hidden these things from the wise and understanding and revealed them to babes" (Matt. 11:25), did he not truly confound the proud and lift up those who were lowly in their eyes and in the eyes of others?

Mary herself is an example of such a person; he raised her above all others because she declared herself to be the lowest of all creatures. When he made for himself a dwelling place on earth, it was not in the palaces of kings. He chose poor, humble parents and all that the world disdained in order to cast down its pomp. This was the proper character of divine power in the new alliance: to make its virtue felt by its very weakness.

"He has filled the hungry with good things, and the rich he has sent empty away" (Luke 1:53). And when? Was it not when he said: "Blessed are they who hunger ... for they shall be satisfied. Woe to you who are satisfied, for you shall hunger" (cf. Luke 6:21, 25). It is here that we must say with Mary: my soul magnifies the Lord, and exults only in his power, which will be seen in infirmity and lowliness.

It is when God alone remains great that the soul finds peace.

26

He Remembered the Promises
He Spoke to Abraham

Palaces and thrones have been cast down and hovels lifted up. The false grandeur of the world has been destroyed as a universal effect of the birth of Christ from Mary. Yet will she say nothing of the redemption of Israel, of the lost sheep of the tribe of Israel, for whom the Son told us he had come?

Let us listen to the end of the divine canticle: "He has helped his servant Israel" (Luke 1:54). Not on account of the supposed merits of the presumptuous; on the contrary, he laid low the pomp of the Pharisees and the proud thoughts of the doctors of the law. He received Nathanael, a true Israelite, straightforward, without presumption, without mask or guile. Such were the Israelites he helped, those who did not place their confidence in themselves, but instead in his great mercy. "He remembered the promises he spoke to Abraham and to his posterity," promises that will endure "for ever" (cf. Luke 1:54-55).

How happy we are that God has deigned to bind himself to us by promises. He might have given us all that we needed, but by what necessity should he have promised these things to us? Unless it was because he wished, as Mary said, for his mercy to endure from age to age, by saving us through his gift and our fathers by their expectation of it. Let us then attach ourselves with Mary to the unchanging promises of the God who gave Jesus Christ to us. Let us say with Elizabeth: "Happy are we to have believed that what was promised to us would be fulfilled." If the promise of Christ was accomplished after so many centuries, can we doubt that the rest shall be accomplished at the end of the ages? If our fathers before the Messiah believed in him, how much more ought we, who have Jesus Christ as the guarantee of these promises, to believe? Let us abandon ourselves to these promises of grace, to these blessed hopes, and let us quench within us all of the deceitful hopes by which the world makes sport of us.

"We are the true children of the promise; children according to faith, and not according to the flesh" (cf. Gal. 4:28; Rom. 9:7-8), who were shown to Abraham not in the person of Ishmael, nor in the other children who came forth from Abraham according to the laws of flesh and blood, but in the person of Isaac, who came according to the promise, by grace and a miracle. Abraham believed, "fully convinced that God was able to do what he had promised" (Rom. 4:21). He says not only that he foresees what will happen, but also that he will do what he had promised. He had promised children to Abraham according to faith, and so he will give them. We are his children according to faith. He has made us children of faith and grace, and we owe him this new birth. If God made us by grace according to his promise, it was not by our works, but by his mercy that we have been born and regenerated. We are those whom Mary saw when she saw Abraham's posterity. We are those to whose salvation she consented when she said, "Let it be done to me according to your word" (cf. Luke 1:38). She carried all of us in her womb with Jesus Christ, in whom we were.

Let us then sing of her blessedness with our own. Let us proclaim that she is blessed and join ourselves to those who look upon her as their mother. Let us pray to this new Eve, who healed the wound of the first, to show us — in the place of the forbidden fruit that brought about our death — the blessed fruit of her womb. Let us unite ourselves to the holy canticle in which Mary sang of our future deliverance. Let us say with Saint Ambrose:

He Remembered the Promises

"May Mary's soul be in us to exalt the Lord; may Mary's spirit be in us to rejoice in our Savior." Like Mary, let us find our peace in seeing the waning glory of the world and the rising kingdom of God and the fulfillment of his will.

27

Mary Stayed with Elizabeth for Three Months

"Mary remained with her about three months, and returned to her home" (Luke 1:56). Charity must not be fleeting. Mary stayed with Elizabeth for three months. Whoever bears grace should not go running about, but should allow time for grace to achieve its work. It was not enough for the babe to leap once in the womb, nor for Elizabeth to have exclaimed, "Blessed are you." It was necessary that the attraction of grace be strengthened, and this was what Mary did, or rather what Jesus did, by staying for three months with his precursor.

Let us ponder this holy precursor, sanctified in his mother's womb. Like the rest of us, he was conceived in sin, but Jesus Christ wanted to make him holy before his birth. Jesus wanted John to enter into his office from his mother's womb. We must not be astonished to see John the Baptist so closely tied to Jesus from the very beginning of the Gospel of Saint John. John the Baptist, who was not the light, nevertheless had the task of bearing witness to the still-hidden light, and even before his birth (John 1:8). He was not the light, inasmuch as he was conceived in sin and awaited the presence of the Savior to be redeemed.

"The true light that enlightens every man was coming into the world" (John 1:9). It was by this light that John was illuminated, so that we might understand that he shows Jesus Christ to the world by the light that he receives from Jesus Christ himself. O Mary! O Elizabeth! O John! Such great things you show to us today. But O Jesus, hidden God, who without appearing accomplish everything on this holy day, I adore you in this mystery and in all the hidden works of your grace!

Whether the Virgin saw the birth of Saint John the Gospel did not wish to tell us. Elizabeth was in her sixth month when Mary came to visit her, and Mary stayed about three months. Elizabeth was, then, at her term or close to it. The Gospel adds that "the time of Elizabeth was accomplished" (cf. Luke 1:57), suggesting, according to some, that it was fulfilled while Mary was with her. Yet who will dare to say for certain when the Gospel seems to have avoided declaring it? Either Mary, devoted to her solitude and anticipating the arrival of a great crowd at the time of the birth, took her leave beforehand, or, if she stayed with all the others, she remained there humble and hidden and unknown, without being noticed amidst the great gathering and content to have accomplished God's wishes for those to whom she had been sent. O the humility! O the silence! It was a silence interrupted only by a song inspired by God. May I imitate her silence all my life.

28

The Birth of John the Baptist

"Now the time came for Elizabeth to be delivered and she gave birth to a son. And her neighbors and kinsfolk heard that the Lord had shown great mercy to her, and they rejoiced with her" (Luke 1:57-58).

True gatherings of the friends and families of Christians should have for their object to celebrate the mercy that God has shown to us. Without this object, the congratulations we receive have nothing solid or sincere about them and are vain things.

God weaves the fabric of his designs in a wonderful order. He intended the birth of John the Baptist to be renowned and the birth of his Son to be celebrated in the prophecy of Zechariah. It was important to the plan of God that the one he would send to announce his Son to the world should be famous from his birth. So here, under the pretext of ordinary civility, God gathers together those who would be the witnesses of the glory of John the Baptist, those who would speak of and remember his birth. For all of them were amazed, and the miracles that were seen at his birth "were talked about through all the hill country of Judea; and all who heard them laid them up in their hearts, saying, 'What then will this child be?' For the hand of the Lord was with him" (Luke 1:65-66). Let us accustom ourselves to noting that the actions that seem most ordinary are secretly directed by the order of God and serve his designs without our noticing it, in such a way that nothing comes to pass by mere coincidence.

"On the eighth day they came to circumcise the child; and they would have named him Zechariah after his father, but his mother said, 'Not so; he shall be called John.' And they said to her, 'None of your kindred is called by this name.' And they made signs to his father, inquiring what he would have him called. And he asked for a writing tablet, and wrote, 'His name is John' " (Luke 1:59-63). This decision gave all to understand that the name had come from above. "And fear came on all their neighbors" (Luke 1:65). The name *John* signifies grace, piety, and mercy. God predestined this name for the precursor of his grace and mercy.

It appears that Zechariah, to whom they spoke by signs, had become not only mute by his incredulity, but that the angel had also struck him deaf. Yet his hearing was

The Birth of John the Baptist

restored to him at the same time as his power of speech, when he had obeyed the angel by giving his son the name *John*. Obedience thus cured the evil that had been caused by his lack of faith.

29

Blessed Be the Lord,
the God of Israel

"Blessed be the Lord God of Israel" (Luke 1:68). After having been speechless for so long, Zechariah suddenly cries out to express the marvel that Christ had come and would soon appear. He proclaims what he sees, and he sees at the same time the part that his son will play in this great work.

This testimony of a priest renowned among his people, and as wise as he was pious, was spoken to give glory to Jesus Christ. All the words of his canticle testify to the promises made to our fathers and to the prophets of old.

He begins by blessing God: "for he has visited and redeemed his people," by sending them his Son, in whom "he has raised up a horn of salvation for us, in the house of his servant David" (cf. Luke 1:68-69). See how the whole world knew that the Son of Mary came forth, through her, from David and inherited his royalty. The word *horn* is one of magnificence and terror that in Scripture signifies at once glory and an incomparable power for defeating our enemies. This is the task of the Savior born of David for the redemption of mankind.

The holy priest makes us see two things in this redemption: the first are the evils from which it frees us, and the second are the graces that it brings us.

To the first, then: "as he spoke by the mouth of his holy prophets from of old, that we should be saved from our enemies and from the hand of all who hate us" (Luke 1:70-71). Who are the enemies from whom we need to be delivered? They are, in the first place, the invisible enemies who hold us captive by our sins, our vices, and all our evil desires. These are our true enemies, the only ones that can bring about our perdition.

Jesus Christ also delivers us from visible enemies by his teaching. We ought to fear them, but conquer them by charity and patience, according to Saint Paul's saying: "Do not be overcome by evil, but overcome evil with good," being careful to win over by your charity your brothers who persecute you, "heaping coals upon their heads" to warm up and melt their icy, hardened hearts (Rom. 12:21, 20).

This is the way the Savior has taught us to vanquish our enemies. Yet if it is necessary that they be vanquished openly, God will put them at our feet in another way, as he did with the persecuting tyrants of Egypt.

When God allows his people to prosper against enemies who oppress them, they should look upon this happy success as a grace and profit from it in order the better to serve God. If, however, they abuse it by leading a licentious life, their peace is no holy and Christian peace, but a scourge more terrible than war itself.

Yet the true enemies whose defeat has been promised by the Savior are the demons, our conquerors since the beginning of the world; our desires, which make war in our members; our sins, which overwhelm us; our weaknesses, which kill us; the terrors of our conscience, which give us no rest. These are the true evils from which Jesus Christ delivers us to make us walk without fear in his presence (Luke 1:74).

It does not suffice to deliver us from evils. The reign of Jesus Christ brings us holiness, which should have two qualities. The first is expressed by these words: "that we might serve him in holiness and righteousness before him" (Luke 1:74-75); that is to say, in a perfect and true holiness not in the eyes of men, but in the eyes of God. For the reign of Jesus Christ is not a question of exterior purifications, or of vain ceremonies, or of superficial justice. We must be entirely holy; we must maintain ourselves in the sight of God and do everything for the one who sounds the depths of our hearts, and think only of pleasing him. That is not enough, however: we must also persevere in this estate. No fleeting virtue is worthy of Jesus Christ. Those who, moved by the sweetness of newfound devotion, fall back at the first temptation are the "rocky ground" (Mark 4:16), because they are righteous only for a time. The proof of a true Christian is perseverance, and the grace that Jesus Christ brings to us is a grace that makes us truly just before God and also makes us persevering, walking both humbly and with courage in the sight of God throughout the whole of our lives.

Let us begin a new life under the reign of Jesus Christ. Let us be just in his sight, exterminating for the love of him every stain that would offend his regard and practicing a firm and austere virtue that never retreats for any reason.

30

The Mercy Promised
to Our Fathers

"To perform the mercy promised to our fathers, and to remember his holy covenant, the oath which he swore to our father Abraham" (Luke 1:72-73): it seems needful to say that God exercises his mercy upon us in memory of our fathers. To disabuse us of any confidence in our own justice, and to make us better understand that we are saved by grace, the holy priest Zechariah prefers to say that God performs his mercy toward our fathers who have pleased him rather than to their ungrateful children, that God saves us by his goodness and not according to our merits, that is, to satisfy his promise rather than to repay our works, which are so evil.

We must believe that the merits of the saints are graces from God. The grace that gives good works to us is given without our meriting it. When one is holy, one has merit. Yet, to be holy, there must first be a promise made from God's pure goodness. The reward is indeed due to those who do good works; but the grace—which is not merited—precedes those good works and enables them to be done. Children of grace and of the promise, live in this faith: it is the new alliance that God has made with us, "so that no human being might boast in the presence of God," and so that he "who boasts, [boasts] of the Lord" (1 Cor. 1:29, 31).

According to "the oath which he swore to our father Abraham"—the mystery of these words cannot be better expressed than by the letter to the Hebrews. "When God made a promise to Abraham, since he had no one greater by whom to swear, he swore by himself" (Heb. 6:13). Thus it is written: "By myself I have sworn, says the Lord." So Abraham, the apostle continues, "having patiently endured, obtained the promise." For as men "swear by a greater than themselves," and the oath by which they bring the omnipotence and truth of God into their engagement is "in all their disputes ... final for confirmation," so also "when God desired to show more convincingly to the heirs of the promise the unchangeable character of his purpose, he interposed with an oath, so that through two unchangeable things [that is, God's word and the oath that confirmed it], in which it is impossible that God should prove false, we who have fled for refuge might have strong encouragement to seize the hope set before us" (Heb. 6:16-18).

No commentary need be offered here; all we need do is listen to the words and let them penetrate us. Let us only take care that in attaching ourselves to the promise, we do not presume on it. God has promised the remission of sins to the penitent, but he has not promised unlimited patience to those who endlessly tax it.

31

The Prophet of the Most High

"And you, child, will be called the prophet of the Most High" (Luke 1:76), his own prophet, the prophet par excellence, a prophet and "more than a prophet" (Matt. 11:9), as the Savior himself would call him, because not only would he announce the Savior as one who is about to come, but he would point him out to the people as the one who had come. "You will go before the Lord to prepare his ways" (Luke 1:76). Consider how Zechariah speaks of Jesus Christ, calling him the Most High and the Lord; that is to say, in one sole verse he has twice called him God. Here then is the character of the prophecy of John the Baptist, distinctly marked out by Zechariah: to go before the Lord to prepare his way. And this character is taken from two ancient prophecies, one being Isaiah's: "A voice cries in the wilderness: prepare the way of the LORD, make straight ... a highway for our God" (Isa. 40:3; cf. Matt. 3:3; Mark 1:3; Luke 3:4). The other was from

Malachi: "Behold, I send my messenger to prepare the way before me, and the Lord whom you seek will suddenly come to his temple" (Mal. 3:1).

Thus this learned priest explains the mission of his son and its proper character by reference to the prophets. It is "to give knowledge of salvation to his people in the forgiveness of their sins (Luke 1:77). This is the proper ministry of Saint John the Baptist, of whom Saint Paul said, "John baptized with the baptism of repentance, telling the people to believe in the one who was to come after him, that is, Jesus" (Acts 19:4).

Come then to learn this great science, which is the science of salvation. Let us learn that it consists chiefly in the remission of sins, a mercy of which we stand in need our entire lives. Indeed, our justice is more a question of the remission of sins than of the perfection of our virtues.

He is the one who made Saint Paul say, following David: "Blessed are those whose iniquities are forgiven, and whose sins are covered; blessed is the man against whom the Lord will not reckon his sin" (Rom. 4:7-8; Ps. 32:1-2). What we must understand is that not being able to be without sin, our true science is the one that teaches us to purify ourselves more and more every day, by saying with David: "Wash me thoroughly from my iniquity" (Ps. 51:2).

The Prophet of the Most High

This science is in Jesus Christ, of whom it is written: "By his knowledge shall the righteous one, my servant, make many to be accounted righteous; and he shall bear their iniquities" (Isa. 53:11). Thus, it is in Jesus Christ that is found the true science of the remission of sins, which he has expiated by his blood, but John prepared his way to show that it would be in Jesus that our sins would be forgiven.

Let us then spend our whole lives in penitence, inasmuch as the science of our salvation consists in the remission of sins. Let us not glory in a justice as imperfect as our own, for even the most perfect in this life should still fear to be overwhelmed by the multitude of his sins, if he does not take care continually to expiate them by penance and almsgiving. This is the science that Saint John preached when he cried out in the desert, his voice echoing throughout all Judea: "Bear fruit that befits repentance" (Matt. 3:8).

"From the bowels of mercy of our God," *viscera misericordiae:* here alone do we find the remission of our sins (cf. Luke 1:78). Whence it is, Zechariah continues, that "the day shall dawn upon us from on high," *oriens ex alto.* Jesus Christ is the true Orient, the true dawn, "the sun of righteousness" who "shall rise" (Mal. 4:2) "to give light," continues Zechariah, "to those who sit in darkness and in the shadow of death, to guide our feet into the way of peace" (Luke 1:79).

Although you are continually reminded about the on-going need for the remission of sins, do not doubt that justice is infused in your hearts by Jesus Christ. He took the name of *Orient*, or dawn, so that he might show us that he is a light dawning for us. "He was the true light that enlightens every man" (John 1:9). Just as the rising sun dissipates the shadows by spreading forth the light that fills the universe, so also the true Orient, when he comes forth from the bosom of the Father to enlighten us, remits our sins by replacing them with the light of justice, by which we ourselves become light in our Lord. For, as Saint Paul says, "once you were darkness, but now you are light in the Lord" (Eph. 5:8). Not at all in yourselves: it is in Jesus Christ that you learn to walk always with your eyes open and to direct your gaze always toward him, by a good and right intention, from which will follow, in your whole body and your whole person, an eternal light and a luminous torch that enlightens you.

"To guide our feet into the way of peace." O peace, my heart's desire! O Jesus, you who are my peace! You who put me at peace with God, with myself, and with the whole world, and thus make peace both in heaven and on earth! (cf. Col. 1:20). When will it come to pass, O Jesus?

The Prophet of the Most High

When will it come to pass, that by faith in the remission of sins, by the tranquillity of my conscience, by a sweet confidence in your favor, and by an entire acquiescence in your eternal will for all the events of my life—when will I possess this peace?

32

The Virginity of
the Holy Mother of God

"All this took place to fulfill what the Lord had spoken by the prophet [Isaiah]: 'Behold, a virgin shall conceive and bear a son, and his name shall be called Emmanuel (which means, God with us)' " (Matt. 1:22-23).

It is the glory of the Christian Church. What other society has even so much as dared to claim to have for its founder the son of a virgin? So lovely a title never even occurred to the human mind. This glory was reserved for Christianity. It is also the only religion to hold perpetual virginity in honor, to consecrate it to God, and to suffer all sorts of persecutions and even death for it. Jesus Christ declared himself to be the spouse of virgins; he is the one who made known to the world these pure beings, who although previously predicted by the prophets (Isa. 56:3-5), appeared in only the Christian religion. Jesus Christ inspired his apostle to declare that holy virginity is the only condition that can consecrate entirely to God a heart that cannot suffer division (1 Cor. 7:32-35). Son of a virgin, and a virgin himself, he took for his precursor John the Baptist, a virgin, and for his beloved disciple, Saint John, also a virgin according to Christian tradition. His Apostles, who, in order to follow him, left everything behind, including their wives, were always in the company of continence. It is no surprise that holy virginity, like the faith, has had its martyrs. The very persecutors themselves recognized the modesty of the Christian virgins. "We see them," said Saint Ambrose, "brave the instruments of torture but shrink before their eyes; amidst torments and ferocious beasts and angry bulls that threw them into the air, they were careful of modesty, disdaining the torments of life and having bodies of iron but tender countenances." These were worthy witnesses, worthy martyrs of the one who is at once Son of God and son of a virgin.

Son of God and son of a virgin. These two things should go together, so that in every sense it may be said "who will understand his generation?" (cf. Isa. 53:8). The Son was chaste in the bosom of the Father and in the womb of his mother.

O Jesus! We believe it, even if we cannot comprehend it. We know that there is nothing more incompatible than impurity and the Christian religion. Raised amid mysteries so chaste, how could we suffer corruption in our bodies? Does not the very name of Jesus inspire purity in us? Can we even pronounce the name with unclean lips? Can our sentiments be anything but pure when we approach his holy body, the unique fruit of a virgin mother—so pure that he was not able to endure either in himself or in his Mother even the sanctity of the marriage bed?

Sacred ministers of the altar, you must be as pure as the sun. All you Christians, you must detest every impurity. Virgins consecrated to Jesus Christ, his dear spouses, you must be jealous for him and root out every trace of a vice that has so many secret branches. Yet if you would be virgin in both body and soul, humiliate yourselves: love neither the gaze nor the praise of men. Hide yourselves from yourselves, like a modest virgin, who, far from putting herself forward, does not even dare to look upon herself. Christian women, Christian virgins, and you whose celibacy should be the honor of the Church, be careful of a reputation that so greatly edifies the public. Consider that Jesus Christ our high priest, among all the insults he suffered, even to the point of the accusation that he was a "glutton and a drunkard" (Matt. 11:19), never willed that his modesty should have the least stain. "They marveled that he was talking with a woman" (John 4:27), that he conversed with her. He acted in a manner so purified and so serious that, in spite of the wickedness of his enemies, his integrity in this regard remained beyond suspicion. Why did he will this to be the case if it were not for us, so as to make us see how carefully we must conduct ourselves so as to avoid suspicions in a matter so delicate, in which mankind is so easily carried away, so mistrustful, and so curious?

33

He Will Be Called Emmanuel

His name will be Emmanuel: God with us (cf. Isa. 7:14; Matt. 1:23). If we understand the significance of this name *Emmanuel*, we will find it includes the notion of *Savior*. For what is a Savior unless one who takes away sin, just as the angel said? Yet with sins having been taken away and there no longer being any separation between God and us, what remains other than our perfect union with God? We are, then, perfectly and eternally saved, and we recognize in Jesus, the one who saves us, a true Emmanuel. He is the Savior because in him God is with us. He is God united to our nature. Having been reconciled with God, we are lifted up by grace to be one in spirit with him.

This is the work done by the one who is both what God is and what we are: God and man together. "In Christ God was reconciling the world to himself, not counting their trespasses against them" (2 Cor. 5:19). Thus God is with them because they no longer have their sins.

He Will Be Called Emmanuel

This would be nothing, however, were God not also, at the same time, to prevent them from committing new sins. In the style of Scripture, to say that God is with you means that God protects you. God helps you, and with so powerful an assistance that your enemies will not prevail against you. "They will fight against you," says the prophet, "but they shall not prevail against you, for I am with you" (Jer. 1:19). Be with us, O Emmanuel, so that, after the pardon of our sins, when their pernicious attractions and temptations return, we will remain victorious.

Is this the extent of the grace of our Emmanuel? No. Here is a higher one, the final one of all: he will be with us in eternity, when God will be "everything to every one" (1 Cor. 15:28). He will be with us, to purify us from our sins; with us, to lead us to the life entirely free from sin. Here, says Saint Augustine, are three degrees through which we pass in order to gain the salvation we are promised in the name of Jesus and the perfect grace of divine union through our Emmanuel: happy, not only when we will no longer falter under the yoke of our sins, but when we will be free of the temptations that imperil our deliverance!

O Jesus! O Emmanuel! O Savior! O God with us! O victor over sin! O mediator of divine union! With faith I await this blessed day on which you will receive the name of Jesus, the day on which you will be my Emmanuel, always with me, who live amid so many temptations and perils. Protect me with your grace, unite me to yourself, and may all that is in me be subject to your will.

34

The Stable and the
Manger of Jesus Christ

God prepared a great and new spectacle for the world
when he caused a king to be born poor. It was necessary
to prepare a fitting palace and cradle for him. "He came
to his own home, and his own people received him not"
(John 1:11).

There was no place for him when he came. The crowd
and the lords of the earth had filled the inns. All that
Jesus had was an abandoned and deserted stable and a
manger to be laid in (Luke 1:7). It was a fitting shelter
for the one who, when he had come of age, would say:
"Foxes have holes, and birds of the air," that is, the true
nomads of the earth, "have nests, but the Son of man has
nowhere to lay his head" (Luke 9:58). He did not utter
this as a complaint. He was accustomed to this sort of
abandonment; from his very birth he had no place to lay
his head.

He himself willed it to be this way. Let us leave the places inhabited by men. Let us leave the inns where the tumult and the press of the world hold sway. Seek a more simple and innocent retreat for me among the animals. At last we have found a place worthy of the abandoned one. Come out, divine child: everything has been prepared to announce your poverty. He comes forth like a flash of light, like a ray of the sun: his mother is astonished to see him appear all at once. This birth is free from weeping, whether of sorrow or pain. Miraculously conceived, his birth is still more miraculous.

Enter into the possession of your impoverished throne. The angels are coming to adore you upon it. When God introduced you to the world, this commandment came forth from the high throne of his majesty: "Let all God's angels worship him" (Heb. 1:6). Who can doubt that his Mother and his adoptive father also adored him at the same time? It was as a figure of Jesus that Joseph of old had been worshiped by his father and mother (cf. Gen. 37:9-11) but the adoration of Jesus by Mary and Joseph was of an entirely different order, for he was blessed and adored as "the Christ, who is God over all, blessed for ever" (cf. Rom. 9:5).

Do not think to approach this impoverished throne with the love of wealth and high estate. Undeceive yourselves, disabuse yourselves, and dispossess yourselves at least in spirit all you who come to the Savior in the manger. Do we lack the courage to leave everything in order to follow the king of the poor? Let us at least leave everything in spirit, and instead of glorying in the rich belongings that surround us, let us blush for being so pampered when Jesus Christ is naked and abandoned.

And yet he was not naked: his mother "wrapped him in swaddling clothes" with her chaste hands (Luke 2:7). It was necessary to cover the new Adam, whom the air attacked and whom modesty demanded to be clothed. O Mary, cover this tender body and lift him to that virginal breast. Adore him while nursing him. The angels are bringing others to adore him too.

35

The Angels Bring
Good News to the Shepherds

The shepherds, imitators of the holy patriarchs, and the most innocent and guileless men in the world, were "keeping watch over their flock by night" (Luke 2:8). Holy angels, accustomed to conversing with those shepherds of old — with Abraham, Isaac, and Jacob — brought these country folk the news that the Great Shepherd had arrived and that the earth was once again to see a shepherd king, the son of David.

"And an angel of the Lord appeared to them." Let us not, like Manoah the father of Samson, ask the angel his name. He may well also respond to us, "Why do you ask my name, seeing it is wonderful?" (Judg. 13:17-18). Yet do we not hope he is the same angel that appeared to Zechariah and to the Holy Virgin? Be that as it may, without presuming in a place where the Gospel does not speak, let us listen: "An angel of the Lord appeared to them, and the glory of the Lord shone around them, and they were filled with fear" (Luke 2:9).

All divine things initially cause fear in our sinful human nature, banished from heaven as we are. But the angel reassured them, saying, "Be not afraid; for behold, I bring you good news of a great joy." It is in the city of David, he said, this place so long marked out in prophecy, that today is born for you "a Savior, who is Christ the Lord. And this will be a sign for you: you will find a babe wrapped in swaddling clothes and lying in a manger" (Luke 2:10-12). By the singular sign of a child laid in a manger, you will recognize the Christ, the Lord. "For to us a child is born, to us a son is given," who at the very same time is called "Wonderful Counselor, Mighty God, Everlasting Father, Prince of Peace" (Isa. 9:6). "And suddenly there was with the angel a multitude of the heavenly host praising God and saying, 'Glory to God in the highest, and on earth peace' " (Luke 2:13-14).

Here we see a new Lord to whom we belong, a Lord who now receives the supreme and divine name of Christ. This is the God who is the anointed one of God, the one to whom David sang: "God, your God, has anointed you with the oil of gladness above your fellows" (Ps. 45:7). You are God eternally, but you are newly the Christ, God and man at once, and the name of Lord is given to you to express that you are God with the same title as your Father. Henceforward, following the example of the angel, you will be called the Lord in all sovereignty. Command your new people. You do not yet speak, but you command them by your example. And what is that command? To love, or at least to esteem, poverty and to reject the pomp of the world. To seek simplicity, even perhaps the holy rusticity of these new adorers that the angel brings to you and who make up the whole of your courtiers, agreeable to Joseph and to Mary, and appearing like them, for they are equally arrayed with the robe of poverty.

Let us once more consider the angel's words: "You will find a babe wrapped in swaddling clothes and lying in a manger." You will know by this sign that it is the Lord. Go to the courts of kings: you will recognize the newborn prince by his gold-embroidered covers and by a splendid cradle that looks something like a throne. Yet to know the Christ who is born for you, a Lord so high that David his father, although himself a king, called him "my Lord" (Ps. 110:1), all you are given as a sign is the manger in which he is lying, and the poor rags in which his frail infancy has been swaddled. That is to say, all you are given is a nature similar to your own and a poverty below your own. Which of us was born in a stable? Which of us, poor as we may be, gives his child a manger for a crib? Jesus is the only one abandoned to such an extent, and this is the mark by which we are to know him.

If he had wished to make a show of his power, with what gold would his head have been crowned? What purple would have covered his shoulders? What stones would have enriched his vestments? But, as Tertullian tells us, "He judged all this false display, all this borrowed glory, unworthy of him and of his own, and so, in refusing it, he disdained it, and in disdaining it, he proscribed it, and in proscribing it, he placed it with the pomp of the world and the Devil." So it was that our fathers the first Christians were wont to speak, while we wretches breathe only ambition and the love of comfort.

36

The Song of the Angels

"Glory to God in the highest, and on earth peace to men of good will" (cf. Luke 2:14). Peace is announced to the whole world: the peace of man with God by the remission of sins; the peace of men with one another; the peace of man with himself by the accord of all his desires with the will of God. This is the peace that the angels announce to the whole universe.

This peace has as its object the glory of God. Do not rejoice in this peace because of what it makes us feel in our hearts, but because it glorifies God upon the high throne of his glory. Let us rise to the heights, to the greatest height that is the throne of God, to glorify him in himself and to love what he does in us only for his sake.

In this spirit let us sing with the whole Church: *Gloria in excelsis Deo*. Every time this angelic song is intoned, let us enter into the music of the angels by the harmony and concord of all our desires. Let us remember the birth of

The Song of the Angels

our Lord that gave birth to this song. Let us put our hearts into the words that the Church has added to interpret the song of the angels: *Laudamus te, adoramus te* ("we praise you, we adore you"), and most especially, *Gratias agimus tibi, propter magnam gloriam tuam* ("we give you thanks for your great glory"). We love your blessings, because they glorify you, and the good things that you have done for us, because by them your glory is honored.

Peace on earth to men of good will. The word in the original that is here rendered as "good will" signifies the good will of God for us and teaches us that God gives peace to those he cherishes. The original reads, word for word, "Glory to God in the high places, peace upon the earth, good will on the part of God toward men." It is thus that the Churches of the East have always read it. Those of the West come to the same meaning by singing "peace to men of good will," that is to say, in the first place, to those whom God wills the good, and in the second, to those who themselves have a good will, inasmuch as the first effect of the good will of God toward us is to inspire in us a good will toward him.

A good will is one that is in conformity with the will of God. As his will is good in itself, the one who conforms to it is good by that likeness. Let us then rule our will by the will of God. Then we will be men of good will, provided that it not be by insensibility, indolence, negligence, or to avoid work that we "cast all our anxieties upon him" (1 Pet. 5:7) but instead by faith. Our souls become soft and lazy by saying, "Let God do what he will," if we say so in the hope of fleeing pain and anxiety. But truly to be conformed to the will of God, one must know how to make a sacrifice of what is held most dearly and to say to him with a heart that has been torn asunder: "Everything belongs to you; do with it what you will." We must be like the holy man Job who, when he was told the news that he had lost all of his belongings and all of his children in a single day, threw himself on the ground and said: "The Lord gave, and the Lord has taken away; blessed be the name of the Lord" (Job 1:21). The one who adores in this way is the true man of good will, and lifted beyond his senses and his own will, he glorifies God in the high places. This is why he has peace: he labors to calm the trouble in his heart, not because this trouble causes him pain, but because it prevents the perfection of the sacrifice that he wishes to make to God. Otherwise he would only be seeking a false repose. Behold, this is what is meant by good will.

37

The First Proclamation
of the Gospel

The beginning of the Gospel is in the angel's words to the shepherds: "I bring you good news of a great joy," the good news of the birth of a Savior (Luke 2:10). What news could be better? When he first preached in the synagogue after the forty days in the desert, he himself explained the cause of this joy. He spoke the words of Isaiah that he found upon opening the scroll: "The Spirit of the Lord is upon me, because he has anointed me to preach good news to the poor. He has sent me to proclaim release to the captives and recovering of sight to the blind, to set at liberty those who are oppressed, to proclaim the acceptable year of the Lord" (Luke 4:18-19; cf. Isa. 61:1-2). What joy could equal this? And what more could good men wish for than to see God exalted by such wonders? From the Gospel we learn the happy news of our salvation. Learning it, we rejoice in it. We behold God's glory, and we glorify him. Let us rise to the high places, to the sublime part of ourselves; let us rise above ourselves to seek God in himself and, with the angels, to rejoice in his great glory.

After the song of the angels, "the shepherds said to one another, 'Let us go over to Bethlehem,' " and, going in haste, "they found Mary and Joseph and the babe lying in a manger" (Luke 2:15-16). Here then is the Savior who has been announced to us! We sigh over the sign that makes him known! It is a unique poverty. We will never again complain of our own misery. We will prefer our cottages to the palaces of kings. We will live happily under our thatched roofs, roofs too splendid to have sheltered the King of kings. Let us go everywhere and tell this good news. Let us go everywhere to console the poor by telling them the wonders we have seen.

How God has prepared the way for his gospel! Everyone was astonished to hear the beautiful testimony from these innocent although uncouth lips. If it had been famous men—Pharisees or doctors of the Law—who had recounted these wonders, the world would have doubted their intentions, inclining to believe that they had wished to make a name for themselves with their sublime visions. But who would dream of contradicting these simple shepherds in their naïve and sincere testimony? The fullness of their joy shines forth naturally, and their discourse is artless. Witnesses such as these were necessary for the one who would choose fishermen to be his first disciples and the future teachers of his Church.

Every mystery of Jesus Christ wears the same finery. Let us labor to save the poor and to help them to feel the grace of their condition. Let us humble the rich of the world and confound their pride. If something is lacking to us—and who is not lacking for something?—let us love, let us adore, let us kiss the poverty of Jesus Christ. Let us not wish to be wealthy, for what will we gain by it? If we wish to be Christians, we must be ready to detach ourselves and lose everything.

38

The Silent Wonder
of Mary and Joseph

We beheld the shepherds coming in from their fields glorifying God and bringing all who heard them to glorify him too. Yet here is something still more marvelous and edifying: "Mary kept all these things, pondering them in her heart." And furthermore, "his father and his mother marveled at what was said about him" (Luke 2:19, 33). Would it not be better to unite ourselves to Mary's silence rather than to attempt to explain her merits with words? For what is more wonderful, after the annunciation and the birth, than to hear the whole world talking but nevertheless to remain silent? She had carried in her womb the Son of the Most High. She had seen him come forth like a ray of the sun from a cloud, pure and luminous. What must she have felt by his presence? And if only for being near him, John leaped for joy in his mother's womb, what peace and what divine joy were felt by the Blessed

The Silent Wonder of Mary and Joseph

Virgin at the conception of the Word that the Holy Spirit formed in her? What, then, could she have said about her dear Son? Nevertheless, she allows him to be praised by everyone; she listens to the shepherds; she speaks not a word to the Magi who come to adore her Son; she listens to Simeon and to Anna the prophetess; she speaks only to Saint Elizabeth, who had been made a prophet by her visit, while Mary herself appeared only to be astonished and ignorant. Joseph shared in her silence as he shared in her secret, he to whom the angel had spoken such great things and who had seen the miracle of the virgin birth. Neither of them spoke of what they saw every day in their house nor sought any advantage from so many miracles. As humble as she was wise, Mary allowed herself to be thought of as a simple mother and her Son as the off-spring of an ordinary marriage.

The great things that God works within his creatures naturally happen in silence, in a certain divine move-ment that suppresses all speech. For what could we say, and what could Mary have said that could have equaled what she felt? Thus, God's secret is kept under the seal un-less he himself opens the lips and makes the words come forth. Human advantages are nothing if they remain un-known and if the world does not lay hold of them. Those God makes, however, have in themselves an inestimable worth that one wants to share with God alone. Men, how vain you are, and how vain is the ostentation that moves you to make a display of your feeble accomplishments for the eyes of men just as vain as you! "O men, how long will you love vain words, and seek after lies?" (Ps. 4:2). All the goods that one vaunts are nothing in themselves: opinion alone gives them their value. There are no true goods but the ones that can be tasted in silence with God. "Be still, and know that I am God" (Ps. 46:10). "O taste and see that the Lord is good" (Ps. 34:8). Love solitude and silence. Draw back from the noisy conversation of the world. Stay closed, O my mouth, and do not deafen my heart, for it is listening to God. Stop interrupting and troubling my sweet attentiveness. *Vacate et videte*, says the psalmist: "live in holy leisure and see." And again: "Taste and see that the Lord is good." Allow this celestial taste to speak in you. *Gustate et videte, quoniam suavis est Dominus.*

39

The Holy Name of Jesus

"And at the end of eight days, when he was circumcised, he was called Jesus" (Luke 2:21). Jesus suffered himself to be placed in the ranks of sinners. He came like a vile slave to carry upon his own flesh a servile character and the mark of Original Sin. Here he is, then, to all appearances a son of Adam like the others. It was necessary that he too carry the mark of sin, just as he would carry its penalty.

Yet instead of being like us, impure in our origin, he was holy in his origin, conceived by the Holy Spirit, who sanctifies all things, and united in person to the Son of God, who is the Holy of holies in his essence. The Spirit that sanctifies us in our regeneration is the one by which Jesus Christ was conceived, by whom his holy flesh was formed, and who was naturally infused in his holy soul, in such a way that he did not need to be circumcised. He submitted to this law only to fulfill the claims of justice and to give the world an example of perfect obedience.

Nevertheless, by receiving circumcision, he rendered himself, as Saint Paul said, "bound to keep the whole law" (Gal. 5:3). He did this for our sakes, in order to free us from that heavy yoke. Behold us, then, free by the slavery of Jesus: let us walk in the liberty of the sons of God, no longer in a spirit of fear and terror, but in a spirit of love and confidence.

The name of the Savior is a pledge of this confidence for us. Jesus saves us from our sins, just as he said he would, by remitting those we have committed, by helping us to avoid sin, and by leading us to the life in which we will never sin again.

It was "by his own blood" that he "secured us an eternal redemption" (Heb. 9:12). It was necessary that it cost him some blood to receive the name of Jesus. This little bit of bloodshed was the promise that all of it would at last be poured out, and it was the beginning of our redemption. I see, O Jesus, all your veins cut open, your whole body wounded, your head and your side pierced, your blood flowing out in great streams, and yet you hold it back and reserve it for the Cross. Receive, then, the name of Jesus: you are worthy of it, and you have begun its purchase by your blood. Receive this name at which "every knee should bow, in heaven and on earth and under the earth" (Phil. 2:10). The Lamb that sheds its blood deserves to receive all adoration, all worship, all praise, all thanksgiving (cf. Rev. 5:12). I have heard every creature in heaven and on the earth and under the earth cry out with a great voice: "Salvation belongs to our God" (Rev. 7:10).

Salvation comes from him because he sends us the Savior. Hail to the Lamb who is the Savior himself. Hail to us who participate in his name. If he is the Savior, we are the saved, and we carry this glorious name before which the whole universe bends its knee and the demons tremble. Let us not fear anything, for everything is at our feet. Let us think only about conquering ourselves: everything must be conquered, because we are already bearing the victor's name. Take heart, he says, for "I have overcome the world" (John 16:33), and to him "who conquers, I will grant ... to sit with me on my throne" (Rev. 3:21).

40

The Star of the Magi

Behold the first fruits of the blood of Jesus among the Gentiles. "We have seen his star" (Matt. 2:2). What quality of this star made it a herald of the glory of God from the heavens? How was it able to be called the star of the King of kings, of the newborn Christ, and to summon the Magi?

Balaam of Moab, a prophet among the Gentiles, saw Jesus Christ like a star, and he said, "A star shall come forth out of Jacob" (Num. 24:17). This star that appeared to the Magi was the one Balaam had foreseen. Had the prophecy of Balaam been spread throughout the East and Arabia and come to the ears of the Magi? Whatever may have been the case, a star that appeared only to the eyes could not have drawn the Magi to the newborn King; for this, the star of Jacob and the light of Christ must shine in their hearts. In the presence of the sign that shone without, God touched them within by that inspiration of which Jesus spoke: "No one can come to me unless the Father who sent me draws him" (John 6:44).

The star of the Magi is thus an inspiration in the heart. Something unknown shines within you. You are in the darkness and among dissipations, or perhaps even the world's corruption: turn to the East, where the stars arise; turn to Jesus Christ, who is the Orient, where you will see arising like a star the love of virtue and truth. Go forward then; imitate the Magi. "We have seen his star, and we have come" (Matt. 2:2). We saw it, and we started after it. To go where? We still do not know. We begin by leaving our homes. You should leave the world itself, that world for which this new star, this chaste inspiration that burns your heart, begins to give you a secret distaste.

Go to Jerusalem; receive the light of the Church. Go, leave behind your home, or rather, leave the place of your banishment that you take to be your home, because it is in corruption that you were born. From your mother's womb, accustomed to the life of the senses, pass now to another region. There you will find the doctors who will interpret the prophecies for you and help you to understand the plan of God. And you will walk securely, thanks to their direction. Learn to know Jerusalem, and the crèche of your Savior, and the bread that he prepares for you in Bethlehem.

Guard What Has Been
Entrusted to You

A Sermon for the Feast of Saint Joseph

We are all perfectly well aware that to hold something
in trust is to fulfill a sacred duty, one that not only calls
upon our honor, but even requires a kind of religious ob-
servance. Saint Ambrose tells us of the pious custom of
the faithful bringing their most valued possessions to the
bishops and clergy for safekeeping before the altar. Theirs
was a kind of holy intuition that treasures could not be
better kept than where God had placed his own sacred
mysteries. This custom was handed down from the synagogue of old. In the sacred history, we read that the ven-
erable Temple of Jerusalem was a place of safekeeping for
the Jews; from profane writers we learn that the pagans
paid the same honor to their false gods by placing their
treasures in their temples and by confiding them to their

priests. It is as if nature were teaching us that the obligation to keep a trust is a religious one and that precious objects cannot be safer than where the Divinity is revered and in hands consecrated to religion.

Yet if ever there were a trust that was worthy of the name *sacred* and of being guarded in a holy manner, it is the one of which I speak today, the one that the providence of the eternal Father committed to the faith of that just man, Joseph. His very house became a kind of temple that God deigned to inhabit. To guard such a treasure, Joseph himself had to be consecrated. And truly he was, for his body was consecrated by purity and his soul by all the gifts of grace.

O Mary, you saw the effects of the grace that filled him; I need your assistance to make them known. May I not hope for your most powerful intercession when I undertake to praise the chaste spouse chosen by the Father to preserve the purity that was so dear and precious to you? We therefore have recourse to you, O Mary, and greet you with the angel, saying: *Ave, gratia plena.*

In my plan of basing the praise of Saint Joseph not upon doubtful conjectures, but upon a solid doctrine drawn from the Holy Scriptures and the Fathers, I cannot better observe the solemnity of this day than by presenting this great saint to you as a man singled out to guard

Guard What Has Been Entrusted to You

God's treasure and to be his trustee here below. I shall attempt to explain that this worthy title of trustee—a title that unfolds the designs of God for this blessed patriarch—discloses the source of all his graces and the sure foundation of his honor.

It is a simple matter for me to show you how estimable is this quality. For if the name of trustee is a mark of honor and testifies to probity; if, in order to confide a trust, we choose the one whose virtue is most assured, whose fidelity is most proven, and finally, the one who is the most intimate and most confidential of our friends, then how shall we measure the glory of Saint Joseph? God made him the trustee not only of blessed Mary, whose angelic purity made her so acceptable in his eyes, but still more of his own Son, the sole object of his delight and the unique hope of our salvation. Saint Joseph he made the trustee of the common treasure of God and man: the person of Jesus Christ. What eloquence could equal the grandeur and majesty of this title?

He cannot be rightly praised without the assistance of grace. Grace will help me to plumb so deep a mystery and seek in the Scriptures what is said of Joseph, so as to enable you to see that everything may be traced back to this great role of trustee. In the Gospels, I find three things entrusted to Joseph, and I also find three virtues that shine forth, virtues corresponding to those three treasures. These are the matters that must be explained in an orderly way.

The first of the treasures committed to his trust — the first, that is, in the order of time — was the holy virginity of Mary, which he had to preserve inviolate under the sacred veil of marriage, and which he always religiously protected as a sacred trust. The second and the more imposing was the person of Jesus Christ, whom the heavenly Father placed in his hands so that he might serve as the earthly father of the holy child. The third you will find most admirable, if I am able to explain it to you clearly. To understand it, we must realize that a secret is a kind of treasure. To betray the secret of a friend is to violate the sanctity of trust. The law says that if you spread abroad the secret of a testament that I confide in you, I may then take action against you for your lapse as trustee. The reason for this is plain: a secret is a kind of trust. From this you will easily comprehend that Joseph was the trustee of the eternal Father because God told him his secret. Which secret? The marvelous secret of the Incarnation of his Son. God's plan was not to reveal Jesus Christ to the world before his hour had come. Saint Joseph was chosen not only to keep the secret, but even to conceal it. Thus, we read in the Gospel that, with Mary, he marveled at all that was said of the Savior, but we do not read that he spoke, because the eternal Father revealed the mystery to him in secret and under the obligation of silence. Saint Bernard explained: "God desired to entrust to his faithfulness the most sacred secret of his heart."

How precious you are to God, O peerless Joseph, for to you he confided his three great treasures: the virginity of Mary, the person of his only-begotten Son, and the secret of all his mystery.

You must not think that Joseph was ungrateful for these graces. If God honored him by his threefold trust, for his part, in the Gospel, he made an offering to God of the three virtues that I noted. I do not doubt that his life was adorned with all the others; but here are the three principal ones that God presents to us in his Scripture. The first, his purity, is demonstrated by his continence in marriage. Who does not see the purity of Joseph in that holy society of chaste desires and that admirable correspondence with the virginity of Mary in their spiritual wedding? The second was his fidelity. How faithful was his untiring care for Jesus along the many journeys that awaited the holy child from the beginning of his life! The third was his humility. Although the possessor of the greatest of treasures through an extraordinary grace of the eternal Father, far from preening himself on his gifts or publicizing his advantages, he hid himself from mortal eyes as much as possible, peaceably enjoying with God the mystery that God had revealed to him and the infinite riches that God had entrusted to him. Here we are in the presence of greatness, a greatness that offers crucial lessons. There is greatness in these treasures and in the example of these virtues. Let us enter into the heart of the mystery by admiring God's plan for the matchless Joseph. Having seen him entrusted with great cares, having seen his virtues, let us consider the connection of the former with the latter, and let us make this correspondence the division of our discourse.

What virtue did Joseph require in order to protect the virginity of Mary under the veil of marriage? An angelic purity that might in some way correspond to the purity of his chaste spouse. What virtue was required to preserve the Savior Jesus among the many persecutions that attacked him from his infancy? An inviolable fidelity, one that would not be shaken amid peril. And last, what virtue enabled him to keep God's secret? An admirable humility that fears the eyes of men and does not wish to show itself to the world, but instead loves to hide with Jesus Christ.

Depositum custodi: O Joseph, guard what has been entrusted to you. Protect the virginity of Mary, and, to protect it within marriage, join to it your own purity; protect that precious life on which depends the salvation of mankind, preserve it amid so many dangers; protect the secret of the eternal Father, for he wants his Son to be hidden from the world. Be a sacred veil for him and wrap him in the obscurity that covers you, by your love for the hidden life.

These are the points that I propose to explain with the help of grace.

I

In order fully to comprehend the great honor that God accorded to Saint Joseph when he entrusted him with Mary's virginity, we must first understand how precious this virginity is to heaven and how useful it is to the earth. The Holy Scriptures show how necessary this virginity was to bring Jesus Christ to the world. It was the design of providence that just as God had begotten his Son from all eternity by a virginal generation, so also, when he had to be born in time, he came forth from a virgin mother. This is why the prophets had announced that a virgin would conceive a Son; our fathers lived in this hope, and the Gospel has shown to us its blessed fulfillment. If, however, we may be allowed to inquire into the causes of so great a mystery, it seems to me that a weighty one may be found, for by examining the nature of holy virginity according to the teaching of the Fathers, we may note its secret power, a power that in some sense obliged the Son of God to come into the world by its cooperation.

Let us then ask the ancient Doctors in what manner they would define Christian virginity. They reply with one accord that it is an imitation of the life of the angels, that it places men above their bodies by a disdain for bodily pleasures, and that it elevates the flesh so much that, if we may say so, it comes to equal the purity of the spirit. Teach us, O great Augustine; let us hear of your high regard for virgins. Here is a lovely phrase: *Habent aliquid jam non carnis in carne.* They have in the flesh, he says, something that is not of the flesh, and that belongs more to angels than to men. Virginity, then, is a kind of middle state between the spirit and the body; it brings us nearer to spiritual beings.

It is now easy to comprehend why this virtue should have preceded the mystery of the Incarnation. For what is the mystery of the Incarnation? It is the intimate union of God with man, of Divinity with flesh. "The Word was made flesh," says the Evangelist; here is the union, here is the mystery. Yet does it not seem that there is too great a disproportion between the corruption of our bodies and the immortal beauty of that pure spirit? Can it be possible to unite natures that are so far apart? It is for that reason that holy virginity was placed between the two, so as to bring them together by its mediation. Light falling upon opaque bodies cannot penetrate them, but seems on the contrary to retreat by reflecting back upon its own rays; yet light enters and unites itself to a transparent body, because in it the light finds the brilliance and the transparency that approach its own nature and contain something of light. In a similar way, we may say that the divinity of the eternal Word, wanting to unite itself to a mortal body, demanded the blessed mediation of holy virginity, which, having in it something spiritual, was in some sense able to prepare the flesh to be united to this pure spirit.

I do not speak of this matter on my own authority. Learn this truth from a famous bishop of the East, the great Gregory of Nyssa. "It is virginity that makes God not refuse to dwell with men and that gives men their wings on which to fly heavenward. As a sacred bond of friendship between man and God, it brings together by its mediation things that are far removed from one another by their natures."

Could the truth that I am preaching be confirmed with greater clarity? Do you not see in it the worthiness of both Mary and of Joseph, her faithful spouse? You see the worthiness of Mary, for her blessed virginity was chosen from all eternity to give Jesus Christ to the world. And you see the worthiness of Joseph, for Mary's purity — so essential to mankind — was confided to his care; thus, he preserved what was most necessary to the world.

O Joseph, guard what has been entrusted to you. *Depositum custodi*. As it pleased the eternal Father to guard Mary's virginity under the veil of marriage, it could no longer be preserved without you, and thus your purity has in some sense become necessary to the world, by the glorious charge that was given to you to protect the purity of Mary.

At this point we must consider the celestial marriage, designed by providence to protect virginity and by this means to give Jesus Christ to the world. Who should I take as a guide in this difficult subject if not the incomparable Augustine, who has treated of this mystery in so divine a manner? Listen to this wise bishop and attend closely to his thoughts. He first remarks that in marriage there are three bonds. There is the sacred contract by which those who are united give themselves to one another without reserve. Second, there is the conjugal love by which they mutually vow hearts that can no longer be divided and that can burn with no other passion. Third, there are the children. The love of the parents is strengthened by seeing itself in the common fruit of the marriage.

Saint Augustine finds these three things in the marriage of Saint Joseph, and he shows us that they all contribute to protecting his virginity. In the sacred contract by which they were given to one another is the triumph of purity. For Mary belonged to Joseph, and Joseph to the divine Mary, and their marriage was most true because they gave themselves to one another. How? Purity, here is your triumph. Each ceded the right to guard their purity to the other. Yes, Mary had the right to guard Joseph's virginity, and Joseph had the right to guard Mary's. These are the promises that brought them together; this was the treaty that bound them. Two virgins united themselves in order that each might preserve the other eternally by the chaste correspondence of their modest desires. It is as though we were seeing two stars enter into conjunction only by the alignment of their lights. Therefore the bond of this marriage, says Saint Augustine, is all the more firm: the promises they made to one another were the more unshakable for the very reason that they were the more holy.

Who now can describe the conjugal love of these blessed married ones? For, O holy virginity, your flames are all the stronger to the extent that they are purer and more detached; and the fire of concupiscence, which is burning in our bodies, can never equal the ardor of the chaste embraces of these spirits bound together by the love of purity. I seek no reasons to prove this truth; I shall found it upon a great miracle I have read about in Saint Gregory of Tours, in the first book of his *History*. The retelling will please or at least refresh you. He tells us that a man and woman from the highest nobility of Auvergne, having lived in marriage with perfect continence, passed over to a happier life and that their bodies were buried in two places some distance apart. But a strange thing happened. It seemed that they could not long endure such a severe separation, and everyone marveled to see their tombs suddenly brought together without anyone having laid a hand to the work. What does this miracle signify? Does it not seem to you that these chaste dead sorrowed to see themselves separated? Does it not seem to you that they are saying to us (permit me to bring them to life and to lend them a voice — God, after all, has permitted them to move), "Why did they bury us apart? We were together for so long, and we were like the dead, because we had extinguished every sentiment of mortal pleasure, and as we were so long accustomed to be together like the dead, death ought not to separate us." God allowed them to be reunited to show us in this miracle that the loveliest flames are not those in which concupiscence is mixed; but those produced by two virgins united in spiritual marriage can, it seems, last even unto the very ashes of death. That is why Gregory of Tours, who narrated this history for us, added that the people of this country called these tombs the tombs of the two lovers, as if the people had wished to say that they were true lovers because they loved by the spirit.

Yet even so spiritual a love was not as perfect as the marriage of Saint Joseph. The love in his union was entirely celestial, because all of his passions and all of his desires were directed to the preservation of virginity. This truth may be easily understood. Tell us, O divine Joseph, what it is that you love in Mary? Doubtless not mortal beauty; it was that hidden and interior beauty, whose principal ornament was holy virginity. It was, therefore, the purity of Mary that was the object of his chaste passion; and the more he loved this purity, the more he wished to guard it, first in his holy spouse, and secondly in himself, by a complete union of hearts. How marvelous it is that everything in this marriage works to uphold the sacred trust. Their promises are wholly pure; their love is wholly virginal. It remains now to consider the greatest marvel: the sacred fruit of the marriage, Jesus the Savior.

You must be astonished to hear me preach with such assurance that Jesus was the fruit of this marriage. Of course, you may say, the incomparable Joseph was the father of Jesus Christ through his care for him; but we also know that he had no part in his blessed birth. How then can you assure us that Jesus was the fruit of this marriage? It may seem impossible, but it is nevertheless true that in a certain sense this blessed infant Jesus came out of the virginal union of these two spouses. For have we not said that it was the virginity of Mary that drew Jesus Christ from heaven? Is not Jesus the blessed flower to which virginity gave the growth? Is he not the blessed fruit that virginity brought forth? Yes, certainly, Saint Fulgence tells us, "he is the fruit, he is the ornament, he is the price and the reward of holy virginity." It was on account of her purity that Mary pleased the eternal Father; it was on account of her purity that the Holy Spirit overshadowed her. May we not then say that it was her purity that made her fruitful? Now, if it was her purity that made her fruitful, I do not fear to assure you that Joseph also had a part in this great miracle. For if that angelic purity was the possession of the divine Mary, it was also entrusted to Joseph the just.

I will proceed still further and tell you that Mary's purity was not only the trust, but also the possession of her holy spouse. Her purity belonged to him by marriage; it belonged to him by the chaste care with which he preserved it. O fruitful virginity! If you were Mary's possession, you also were Joseph's. Mary vowed it, Joseph preserved it, and both of them presented it to the eternal Father as a treasure guarded by their common care. As he had such a part of Mary's holy virginity, he also partook of the fruit that it bore: this is why Jesus is his son, not in truth according to the flesh, but his son by the spirit, thanks to the alliance that joined him to his Mother. Saint Augustine said it with commendable brevity: "on account of this faithful bond, they merited the name parents of Christ." O mystery of purity! O blessed paternity! O incorruptible light, which shines throughout this marriage!

Let us ponder these truths and apply them to ourselves. Everything here was done for love of us; let us then take instruction from what was worked for our salvation. You see how chaste and innocent is the doctrine of Christianity. Shall we never understand who we are? What shame, that we should besmirch ourselves every day by every kind of impurity, we who have been raised in the presence of such chaste mysteries! When shall we understand the dignity of our bodies, whose like the Son of God has taken on? "Let the flesh be taken lightly," said

Tertullian, "or rather, let it be corrupted, before it had been sought out by its master; it was not then worthy of the gift of salvation, nor fit for the office of holiness. It was still, in Adam, tyrannized over by its desires, seduced by apparent beauty, and fastened by the eyes to the earth. It was impure and soiled, because it had not yet been washed in baptism." But God did not want to come into this world as a man unless first drawn by holy virginity—even married holiness was beneath him—and so he wanted to have a virgin mother and he wanted Joseph by his continence to be made worthy to care for him. Since that day on which his blood sanctified life-giving water in order that our flesh might be cleansed of its filth, the flesh is entirely changed. It is no longer that flesh formed from mud and born from concupiscence; it is flesh that has been refashioned and renewed by the purest water and by the Holy Spirit. Therefore, my brothers, let us respect our bodies, which are the members of Jesus Christ; let us keep ourselves from prostituting to impurity this flesh that Baptism has made to be virginal. "Let us possess our vessels in honor, and not in those shameful passions that our brutality inspires in us, as they do in the Gentiles who have no God. For God does not call us to impurity, but to sanctification" in our Lord Jesus Christ (cf. 1 Thess. 4:4-7). By our continence let us honor the holy virginity that gave us the Savior, that rendered his Mother fruitful, and that made Joseph a part of that blessed fecundity, and raised him, if I dare say so, even to being the very father of Jesus Christ. After seeing what he contributed, in a certain way, to the birth of Jesus Christ, let us now see his paternal care, and let us admire the fidelity by which he preserved the divine child whom the heavenly Father had confided to him.

II

It was not enough for the eternal Father to have confided Mary's virginity to Joseph; he prepared something still more exalted for him. Into the hands of this patriarch, he placed Jesus Christ himself. Looking into this secret, into the depths of this mystery, we find so great an honor given to Joseph that we will never be able fully to understand it. For Jesus, whom Joseph always watched and who was the beloved subject of his holy anxiety, was born as an orphan upon this earth and had no father in this world. This is why Saint Paul said that he was without a father: *sine Patre* (Heb. 7:3). It is true that he had one in heaven; yet it seemed that this father had abandoned him and knew him no longer. He would complain of this one day upon the Cross, when he called him his God and not his Father, saying: "Why have you abandoned me?"

(Matt. 27:46). Yet what he said while dying, he could have said from his birth, for from that first moment, his Father exposed him to persecution and abandoned him to injury. All that he did in favor of this only-begotten Son, to show that he had not forgotten him—at least according to what we see—was to place him in the keeping of an upright man who would watch over his painful childhood. It was Joseph who was chosen for this service. What will this holy man do? Who could describe the joy with which he received this abandoned one, and how he offered himself from his whole heart to be the father of this orphan? Thenceforth he lived only for Jesus Christ; he had no care but for him. For this God, he took on the heart and the soul of a father; and what he was not by nature, he became by affection.

Yet we are convinced of the truth of so great a mystery, and one so glorious for Joseph, by the evidence of the Scriptures. Consider this beautiful reflection by Saint John Chrysostom. He notes that in the Gospel, Joseph always appears as a father. He bestowed the name Jesus upon the child, as fathers did in those days. He alone was forewarned by the angel of all of the threats to the child, and the return was announced to him alone. Jesus revered and obeyed Joseph, who directed all of his conduct as having the principal care for it. Whence all this? asks

Chrysostom. Here is the true reason. It was the design of God to give to the great Saint Joseph "everything that could belong to a father without injuring virginity."

I do not know whether I understand the full significance of this thought; but, unless I am mistaken, this is what the great bishop meant. Let us first suppose it to be certain that it was for the sake of holy virginity that the Son of God did not choose a mortal father when becoming man. And because he had to be born of a virgin mother, he could have no father but God. It was virginity, therefore, that prevented Joseph's fatherhood. But this would not preclude Joseph from having the other qualities of a father, says Chrysostom, for holy virginity is opposed only to those qualities that would injure it. In the name of father there are qualities that purity has no difficulty recognizing as her own. Is virginity harmed by care, or tenderness, or affection? See, then, God's secret arrangement, in which Joseph's fatherhood is brought together with virginal purity. "All that belongs to a father without virginity being affected," he says, "this is what I give you." Mary, therefore, will not conceive by Joseph, but Joseph will share all the labors, watching, and anxieties by which Mary will raise the holy Child. And he will feel for Jesus the natural inclination and the tender emotions and feelings of a fatherly heart.

You will perhaps ask where he will find this fatherly heart if nature does not provide it for him? Can these natural inclinations be acquired by choice? Can art imitate what nature writes in the heart? If Joseph be not a father, how will he have a father's love? Here it is that we must acknowledge that a divine power acts in this work. It is by an effect of this power that Saint Joseph has a father's heart, and if nature does not give him one, God makes him one with his own hand. For it is written of God that he turns inclinations where he will. To understand this, we must consider the beautiful theology taught to us by the psalmist when he says that God forms every human heart one by one: *Qui finxit singillatim corda eorum* (Ps. 32:15). Do not believe that David sees the heart as a simple organ of the body that God forms by his power as he does all the other parts of which man is composed. He means something in particular. He considers the heart to be the principle of inclination. And he sees it as soft and moist earth in the hands of God, an earth that yields to and obeys the hands of the potter and receives its shape from them. It is in this way, the psalmist tells us, that God forms each of the hearts of men one by one.

What does this mean, one by one? He fashions a heart of flesh in some, when he softens it by charity, and a hardened heart in others when, pulling back his light in just punishment of their crimes, he abandons them to their reprobate senses. He gives to each of the faithful not the heart of a slave when he sends them the Spirit of his Son, but that of a child. The Apostles first trembled at the least peril; but God made them entirely new hearts, and their courage became invincible. What was Saul's cast of mind while he tended his flock? Doubtless, low and common. Yet in placing him on the throne, God changed his heart by his anointing — *Immutavit Dominus cor Saul* (cf. 1 Kings 10:9) — and he recognized immediately that he was a king. For their part, the Israelites considered this new monarch to be a man from the dregs of the people, but the hand of God touched their hearts as well — *quorum tetigerat Deus corda* (1 Kings 10:26) — and at once they recognized his greatness, and in looking upon him, they were moved by that respectful fear that one has for one's sovereign. God had placed in them the hearts of subjects.

It is the same hand that forms the hearts of men one by one who placed a father's heart in Joseph and a son's heart in Jesus. This is why Jesus obeyed, and why Joseph did not fear to command him. Whence the boldness to command his Creator? The true father of Jesus Christ, the God who begot him in eternity, chose holy Joseph to serve as the father for his only-begotten Son in time and caused his veins to flow with a certain ray or spark of his infinite love for his Son. He changed his heart; he gave him a father's love. And Joseph, who sensed in himself a paternal heart, formed by the very hand of God, also sensed that God had ordained him to employ paternal authority; and thus, he dared to command the one whom he recognized as his master.

And after all of this, need I explain Joseph's fidelity in guarding this sacred trust? Could he have been wanting in fidelity toward the one whom he recognized as his only son? I would not have to speak about this virtue were there not need for such a compelling example of it. For here we learn, by the continual journeys that were required of Saint Joseph once Jesus Christ was placed under his protection, that this trust cannot be preserved without effort, and that, to be faithful to grace, one must be prepared to suffer. Yes, certainly, when Jesus came into a place, he brought his Cross, he carried with him all of his spines, and he shared them with those he loved. Joseph and Mary were poor, but they did not yet lack a home. They had a roof over their heads. As soon as this child came into the world, there was no more home for them, and their shelter was a stable. Who brought this disgrace upon them, if not the one of whom it is written that "coming into his own, his own did not receive him" (John 1:11) and "he had no sure refuge where he might lay down his head" (Matt. 8:20)? Did not their poverty suffice? Why should he bring them persecution? They lived together in their home, in poverty but with sweetness, overcoming their poverty by their patience and hard work. Yet Jesus did not grant them any rest: he came into the world only to trouble them and brought a train of sorrows in tow. Herod could not suffer the child to live; the circumstances of Christ's lowly birth could not conceal him from the tyrant's jealousy. Heaven itself betrayed the secret by pointing out Jesus Christ with a star and by bringing adorers from afar, seemingly only to incite a pitiless persecutor.

What will Saint Joseph do now? Picture for yourselves a poor artisan. His hands are his only inheritance. He has no wealth beyond his workshop, no income beyond what his labor provides. He is forced to go to Egypt and to suffer a troublesome exile, and why? Because he has Jesus Christ with him. Does he complain about this difficult child, who tears him away from his homeland and brings torment upon him? On the contrary, he counts himself happy to suffer in his company; all that troubles him is the peril of the divine Infant, more dear to him than his own life. Does he hope that he will soon see the end of his disgrace? No, he does not expect it; suffering everywhere awaits him. Simeon warned him of future sufferings for his dear Son; he has already witnessed their beginning and will spend his life in continual worry about what lies ahead.

As though his fidelity were unproven, here is a trial yet more troubling. Jesus himself became his persecutor. He cleverly escaped from his hands, hid himself from his oversight, and remained lost for three days. What have you done, faithful Joseph? What has become of the sacred trust that the heavenly father confided in you? Who can tell the tale of your suffering cries? If you have not yet understood Joseph's fatherhood, look upon his tears, look upon his sorrows, and recognize that he is a father. Mary had ample cause to say at the reunion with Jesus: *"Pater tuus et ego dolentes quarebamus te:* Your father and I were searching for you with great sorrow" (cf. Luke 2:48). "O my Son!" she says to the Savior, "I do not fear to call him your father, and by doing so I bring no harm to the purity of your birth. It is on account of his cares and worries that I may call him your father, for he has a truly paternal anxiety: *Ego et pater tuus.* He is joined to me by our common sorrow."

See by what suffering Jesus tests fidelity and how he only wants to be with those who suffer. Soft and voluptuous souls: this child does not wish to abide with you. His poverty is ashamed of your wealth, and his flesh—destined for so much torture—cannot endure your extreme softness. He seeks those strong and courageous ones who will carry his Cross, who will not blush to be the companions of his poverty and misery.

I leave it to you to meditate upon these holy truths. I feel myself called elsewhere and must consider the secret of the eternal Father that was confided to Joseph's humility. We must see Jesus Christ hidden, and Joseph hidden with him, and let the beautiful example inspire in us a love of the hidden life.

III

Where shall I find a light bright enough to shine through the darkness that surrounds the life of Joseph? What have I undertaken, to wish to bring to the light of day what Scripture has covered with a mysterious silence? As it was the design of the eternal Father that his Son be hidden in the world and that Joseph be hidden with him, let us revere the secrets of his providence without seeking to understand them; and let the hidden life of Joseph be the object of our veneration, not the subject of our discourse. All the same, it must be spoken of, and it will be useful for the salvation of souls to meditate upon such a beautiful subject. If nothing else, I will at least say that Joseph had the honor to spend every day with Jesus Christ; that, together with Mary, he had the greater part of his son's graces; that nevertheless Joseph was hidden, that his life, his actions, and his virtues were unknown. Perhaps from so fine an example we will learn that one can be great without outward show, that one can be blessed without attracting attention, and that one can have true glory without the help of fame, but by the testimony of conscience alone: "*Gloria nostra haec est, testimonium conscientiae nostrae*" (2 Cor. 1:12). This thought will inspire us to set at naught the glory of the world.

Yet in order that we may rightly understand the grandeur and dignity of Joseph's hidden life, let us return to the source and first admire the infinite variety of the counsels of providence in the different vocations. Among all of the vocations in the Scriptures, two seem directly opposed: that of the Apostles and that of Joseph. Jesus is revealed to the Apostles and to Joseph, but in a contrary set of conditions. He is revealed to the Apostles in order to be announced to the whole world. He is revealed to Joseph in order to be kept quiet and hidden. The Apostles are lights by which the world may see Christ; Joseph is a veil to cover him, and under this mysterious veil is hidden Mary's virginity and the majesty of the Savior of Souls. And so we read in the Scriptures that when men wished to insult him, they said: "Is this not the son of Joseph?" (John 6:42). In the hands of the Apostles, Jesus is a word that must be preached: "Preach the word of this Life" (Acts 5:20). In the hands of Joseph, Jesus is a hidden word that is not permitted to be revealed: *Verbum absconditum* (Luke 18:34). Consider what follows. The holy Apostles preach the gospel so loudly that the sound of their preaching echoes even unto heaven. Joseph, on the other hand, witnessing the marvels of Jesus Christ, listens, admires, but speaks not a word.

What does this difference mean? Does God contradict himself in these opposing vocations? No. All this diversity tends to teach the children of God one important truth: that Christian perfection consists in nothing but self-surrender. The one who glorified the Apostles by the honor of preaching also glorified Saint Joseph by the humility of silence, and from this fact we should learn that the glory of Christians lies not in brilliant achievements, but in doing what God wants of them. If we may not all have the honor of preaching Jesus Christ, we may all have the honor of obeying him. That is the glory of Saint Joseph, and it is the solid honor of Christianity. Do not ask, therefore, what Saint Joseph did in his hidden life. It is impossible to say, and I can respond only with the words of the holy psalmist: "The just, what has he done? *Justus autem quid fecit?*" (Ps. 11:3). Ordinarily the life of sinners attracts more attention than that of the just, because the passions and the interests are what move the world. The sinners, says David, have bent their bows; they have loosed them against the just; they have destroyed; they have conquered. They are the only ones spoken of in the world: *Quoniam quae perfecisti destruxerunt* (Ps. 10:4). But the just, he adds, what has he done? *Justus autem quid fecit?* He means that the just has done nothing. Indeed, he has done nothing in the eyes of men because he has done everything in the eyes of God. It was in this way that Joseph the just man lived. He saw Jesus Christ and was silent. He heard him and did not speak. He contented himself with God alone, without sharing his glory with men. He accomplished his vocation, for just as the Apostles were the ministers of Jesus Christ revealed, so Joseph was the minster and the companion of his hidden life.

We might wonder why it was necessary that Jesus hide himself, why that eternal splendor of the face of the heavenly Father should cover itself with voluntary darkness for thirty years? Proud men! Have you no idea? Men of the world, do you not know? Your ignorance stems from your pride, from your vain desire to be seen, from your infinite ambition, and from that culpable amiability that makes you shamefully devote to the effort to please men what should be employed to please God. This is why Jesus hides himself. He sees the disorder, he sees the ravages that this sin causes in our minds, and he watches it corrupt our entire lives from childhood until death. He sees the virtues that it suffocates by a low and shameful fear of appearing to be wise and devout; he sees the crimes that it commits, either in order that we may accommodate ourselves to society by a damnable agreeableness, or to satisfy ambition, for the sake of which one sacrifices everything else in the world. But this is not all. He sees that this desire to be seen destroys the highest virtues by making them substitute worldly glory in place of heavenly, by making us do for the love of men what ought to be done for the love of God. Jesus Christ sees all these evils, and he hides himself, in order to teach us to set at naught the noise and show of the world. He does not think that his Cross suffices to conquer the fury of this desire; he chooses, if it were possible, a lower condition, one in which he is in a certain sense even more annihilated.

For in the end I shall not fear to say it: my Savior, I recognize you better upon the Cross and in the shame of your suffering than I do in this lowliness and this unknown life. Even though your body be entirely torn to shreds, your face all bloody, and, far from appearing to be God, you lack the very form of a man, all the same you are not so well hidden from me, and I see, through all of these clouds, a certain ray of your majesty in this constant resolution by which you overcome the greatest of torments. Your sorrow has its dignity; even one of those punished alongside you adores you. But here, I see only what is lowly; and in this state of annihilation, one might declare that you do injury to yourself because it seems that you do nothing. Yet Jesus does not refuse this shame, for it is his will that this injury be added to all the others he has suffered, so that in hiding himself in Nazareth, he might teach us by this great example, that if he should one day show himself to the world, it will be from the desire to aid us and to obey his Father. And that all greatness consists in conforming ourselves to God's orders, however it may please him to dispose of us; and, finally, that this obscurity that we so fear, but that is so illustrious and so glorious, may be chosen even by God. This is what Jesus Christ teaches us, hidden with his humble family, with Mary and Joseph, whom he joins to the obscurity of his life because they are very dear to him. Let us then take our part with them and hide ourselves with Christ.

He is still hidden. He suffers every day because his name is blasphemed and his gospel mocked, because the hour of his greatest glory has not yet come. He is hidden with his Father, and, as the holy apostle says, we are hidden in God with him. As we are hidden with him, it is not in this place of exile that we should seek his glory. But when Jesus shows himself in his majesty, it will then be the time to appear: "*Cum Christus apparuerit . . . tunc et vos apparebitis cum ipso in gloria*" (Col. 3:4). O God! How sweet it will be to stand forth on that day when Jesus will praise us before his holy angels, before the whole universe, and before his heavenly Father. Let men be eternally silent about us, so that Jesus Christ may speak of us on that day.

Let us nevertheless fear that terrible word that he spoke in his Gospel: "You have received your reward" (Matt. 6:2). You desired human glory. You have had it; you are well paid. There is nothing left for you to expect. O ingenious envy of our enemy, who gives us the eyes of men so as to take away those of God; who, by a malicious gratitude, offers to reward our virtues, believing that God will not then reward them. Wretch, I want none of your glory; neither your brilliance nor your vain display can pay me for my work. I await a crown from a hand that is dearer to me, and a reward from a more powerful arm. When Jesus appears in his majesty, then, only then will I stand forth.

It is there, faithful ones, that you will see what I am not able to describe for you today: you will discover the marvels of the hidden life of Joseph. You will know what he did during those long years, and how glorious it is to hide oneself with Jesus Christ. He is, doubtless, not one of those who received his reward in this world. God will repair the obscurity of his life; and his glory will be all the greater for having been reserved for the world to come.

Let us then love the hidden life in which Jesus cloaked himself with Joseph. What does it matter that men see us? The man to whom the eyes of God do not suffice is foolishly ambitious. We do injury to God when we perform for others. If you have had great tasks and important works laid upon you, if it is necessary that your life be a public one, at least meditate seriously on this truth: that in the end your death will be private and your honors will not follow you. May the noise that men make all around you not prevent you from listening to the words of the Son of God. He does not say: Happy are the praised! But he says in his Gospel: Happy are they who are insulted for the love of me (cf. Matt. 5:11). Tremble, then, in whatever earthly glory you attain, lest you be judged worthy of the condemnations of the gospel. Yet if the world refuses to reproach us, let us reproach ourselves before God for our ingratitude and ridiculous vanity. Let us reflect on all of the shame of our life. Let us at least be darkened in our own eyes by a humble confession of our sins, and let us participate as we are able in the shame of Jesus, so that we may participate in his glory. Amen.

Sophia Institute

Sophia Institute is a nonprofit institution that seeks to nurture the spiritual, moral, and cultural life of souls and to spread the Gospel of Christ in conformity with the authentic teachings of the Roman Catholic Church.

Sophia Institute Press fulfills this mission by offering translations, reprints, and new publications that afford readers a rich source of the enduring wisdom of mankind.

Sophia Institute also operates two popular online Catholic resources: CrisisMagazine.com and CatholicExchange.com.

Crisis Magazine provides insightful cultural analysis that arms readers with the arguments necessary for navigating the ideological and theological minefields of the day. *Catholic Exchange* provides world news from a Catholic perspective as well as daily devotionals and articles that will help you to grow in holiness and live a life consistent with the teachings of the Church.

In 2013, Sophia Institute launched Sophia Institute for Teachers to renew and rebuild Catholic culture through service to Catholic education. With the goal of nurturing the spiritual, moral, and cultural life of souls, and an abiding respect for the role and work of teachers, we strive to provide materials and programs that are at once enlightening to the mind and ennobling to the heart; faithful and complete, as well as useful and practical.

Sophia Institute gratefully recognizes the Solidarity Association for preserving and encouraging the growth of our apostolate over the course of many years. Without their generous and timely support, this book would not be in your hands.

www.SophiaInstitute.com
www.CatholicExchange.com
www.CrisisMagazine.com
www.SophiaInstituteforTeachers.org

Sophia Institute Press® is a registered trademark of Sophia Institute. Sophia Institute is a tax-exempt institution as defined by the Internal Revenue Code, Section 501(c)(3). Tax I.D. 22-2548708.